The Way Out of the Pensions Quagmire

The Way Out of the Pensions Quagmire

PHILIP BOOTH AND DEBORAH COOPER

The Institute of Economic Affairs

First published in Great Britain in 2005 by
The Institute of Economic Affairs
2 Lord North Street
Westminster
London SW1P 3LB
in association with Profile Books Ltd

The mission of the Institute of Economic Affairs is to improve public understanding of the fundamental institutions of a free society, with particular reference to the role of markets in solving economic and social problems.

A CIP catalogue record for this book is available from the British Library.

ISBN 0 255 36517 9

Many IEA publications are translated into languages other than English or are reprinted. Permission to translate or to reprint should be sought from the Director General at the address above.

Typeset in Stone by MacGuru Ltd
info@macguru.org.uk

Printed and bound in Great Britain by Hobbs the Printers

CONTENTS

The authors		9
Foreword		11
Summary		13
List of tables and figures		16

1 Introduction 21

Reform must be radical 22
Principles for pension reform 23
A contributory pension not a citizen's pension 28
The Turner Commission 31
Microeconomic, not macroeconomic 33

PART 1: WADING THROUGH THE QUAGMIRE
2 State retirement income provision 37

Basic state pension 37
Second state pension 39
Aspects of the political economy of the contracting-out
   system 43
Means-tested social security benefits in retirement 46
Non-means-tested social security benefits in retirement 48
Total government spending on income provision in
   old age 48

3 Private retirement income provision 50

Occupational pension provision 50

Stakeholder and personal pensions 53

4 Sources of retirement income 57

Differences in income sources across the
income distribution 58

**5 Comparison with retirement income
provision overseas** 62

6 Issues for further analysis 69

PART 2: THE PROBLEMS OF THE QUAGMIRE

**7 Disincentives to save and to work –
means testing** 73

Quantification of the disincentives problem 76

Incentives for early retirement 89

**8 S2P, SERPS and national insurance rebates:
meddling, muddling and work disincentives** 92

Problems caused by rules for contracting out of
SERPS/S2P 96

9 Problems with stakeholder pensions 98

**10 The tax treatment of pension funds and
tax regulations** 103

Alternative tax treatments of savings 103

The tax treatment of pensions in practice 109

The overall tax position   111
Higher-rate tax relief   112
Costs of pension provision under different tax regimes   114
Regulation and the tax system   117

11 The problem of unfunded pensions   121

PART 3: THE WAY OUT OF THE QUAGMIRE
**12 Evaluation of proposals for more
   compulsion**   129
Reasons for not increasing compulsory pension
   provision   134

13 Social security benefits and state pensions   139
Non-cash, non-means-tested benefits   139
Means-tested benefits, social security minimum income
   and the level of compulsory pension provision   140
A new state pension   142
Contracting out and pension scheme regulation   145
An Independent Pensions Commission   151
Benefits of the above reforms   154

14 Changes to the taxation of pensions   156
The taxation of pension funds   156
Administrative reform: reducing the number of tax codes 158
Annuitisation rules   160

15 The retirement age   163
Some economic considerations   163
Removing perverse incentives   164

Deinstitutionalising retirement ages 166

16 Simplifying the taxation of personal income
   in retirement 169

17 Conclusion: The political economy of an end
   to the quagmire 172

Appendix A: Estimate of cost of providing
Minimum Income Guarantee and
Basic State Pension 178
Assumptions 178

Appendix B: Cost of tax regimes 180
Practical problems of TTE and TEE regimes 180
Description of tax regimes 182
Practical difficulties with the comprehensive income
   tax calculations 183
The valuation method and basis 185

References 188

About the IEA 194

THE AUTHORS

Philip Booth

Philip Booth is Editorial and Programme Director at the Institute of Economic Affairs and Professor of Insurance and Risk Management at Sir John Cass Business School, City University. Before joining the IEA he was Associate Dean of Cass Business School and was a special adviser on financial stability issues at the Bank of England. He has published books and journal articles in the fields of social insurance, regulation, investment and finance, and actuarial science. Philip Booth is editor of *Economic Affairs*, published by the IEA, and associate editor of the *British Actuarial Journal*. He is a Fellow of the Institute of Actuaries and a Fellow of the Royal Statistical Society.

Deborah Cooper

Deborah Cooper is Senior Research Actuary at Mercer HR Consulting, working with clients on employee benefit provision and responding on behalf of Mercer on policy issues and government consultations. She is a frequent commentator in the press and professional publications on pensions issues and has published in the professional and academic literature. Before working at Mercer, Deborah Cooper was a Lecturer in Actuarial

Science at City University and also worked at the Government Actuary's Department. She is a Fellow of the Institute of Actuaries and has a PhD from the University of Wales. She is deputy chairman of the Institute of Actuaries' Social Policy Board.

FOREWORD

With concerns about many aspects of the UK pension system, both public and private, growing by the day, there has been no shortage of commentary and criticism on the subject, as well as a number of attempts to propose a way forward. The Pensions Commission, under Adair Turner, has carried out a great deal of analysis of the present structures and has put forward a range of questions to be addressed over the coming months before the commission's final report is due to be published in the latter part of 2005.

The authors of this monograph, Philip Booth and Deborah Cooper, come from very different political perspectives, but they have sought, through careful economic analysis, to identify some of the fundamentals that are needed in designing a sustainable approach going forward, and on which they have discovered they can very largely agree. They lay bare the true nature of many of the features (or perhaps one should say quirks) of the present UK pension scene. These have arisen as the result of unabashed lobbying, at some time in the past, by particular interest groups or as a result of political favours given to appease or woo groups with an identifiable common interest.

Their proposed ideas and solutions are presented as having more or less universal application, rather than being solely for the UK, although inevitably the complications of the current situation and practical politics regarding the possibility of making changes may limit the scope for implementing any such ideal, be it in the UK or in any other country. Nevertheless, the well-considered conclusions, from a closely argued and academically based appraisal of the current complexities and disfunctionalities, do deserve careful study. They offer the opportunity to think where we haven't thought before about radical solutions to pensions problems that would not merely tamper with the symptoms but grapple with the causes of some of the present difficulties facing pensions in the UK.

CHRIS DAYKIN CB, FIA

Government Actuary

December 2004

The views expressed in Research Monograph 60 are, as in all IEA publications, those of the authors and not those of the Institute (which has no corporate view), its managing trustees, Academic Advisory Council members or senior staff. As with all IEA publications, Research Monograph 60 has undergone a thorough process of peer review. As one of the authors is a member of the IEA's staff, the review process was supervised independently by the chairman of the IEA's Academic Advisory Council, Professor Martin Ricketts.

Deborah Cooper is an employee of Mercer HR Consulting. The views expressed in this monograph do not necessarily reflect the views of her employer.

SUMMARY

- The current system of retirement income provision in the UK needs a complete overhaul. This overhaul should not apply just to state pensions but to the tax system surrounding pensions, the social security system, the income tax system for pensioners, the regulation of private schemes and contracting out of the state pension. In many ways the questions asked by Turner's recent Pensions Commission report do not lead to answers that are sufficiently radical.
- The current forms of government involvement in retirement income provision encourage rent-seeking by lobby groups and are the result of effective rent-seeking in the past. The elderly have special tax concessions; pensioners are given a 'tax-free lump sum'; several different forms of social security benefit are given to the elderly, their only apparent purpose being to persuade parts of the electorate to vote in a particular way; regulation and over-complex tax systems provide gains for consultants, regulators and lawyers, who benefit from the complexity.
- The complexity of the current pensions system is also the result of progressive reform to try to mend a broken system and well-intentioned, but failed, initiatives, such as increased means testing.

- In the current pensions system about half of all pensioners are receiving means-tested benefits – a figure that could rise to two-thirds in a generation – and pensioners can often receive about ten forms of income, all with different qualification and tax rules attached to them. The system is ridden with disincentives to save and work.
- Proposals that many pensions researchers, lobby groups and politicians have made for a 'citizen's pension' should be rejected. The contributory principle of the state pension should be retained, as should the principle of contracting out of the state pension system. A 'citizen's pension' system is inherently unstable.
- The state should offer a single, simple, contributory pension benefit, payable from age 70, and a single simple means-tested benefit that does not increase with age. Increased compulsory pension provision is not necessary. Individuals and schemes should be allowed to contract out of the single state pension.
- Such a reform, together with the other reforms we propose, will restore the coherence of the pensions system and restore incentives to save and work – including working beyond state pension age, if an individual desires that.
- There should be no special income tax allowances for the elderly.
- The pension tax-free lump sum should be abolished but pension funds should, once again, be allowed to reclaim corporation tax credits on dividends, thus reversing the '£5 billion a year tax grab'.
- There should be significantly reduced regulation of pension schemes. Solvency should be regulated only in respect of a

small part of the benefits such schemes offer. Regulations surrounding the purchase of annuities should be relaxed significantly.

- An Independent Pensions Commission should be set up. This would have a role in certain technical matters of pension provision to prevent manipulation by politicians. One of its responsibilities would be to set the level of national insurance rebates given to individuals and schemes that are contracted out of the state pension scheme.

TABLES AND FIGURES

Table 1   Current pension scheme membership by age
           and sex   55
Table 2   Individual on median income: sources of
           retirement income   58
Table 3   Return on saving for someone on minimum wage
           saving £20 per month   79
Table 4   Tax regimes   181
Table 5   Assumed asset mix of model scheme   183
Table 6   Net investment returns under different
           tax regimes   183
Table 7   Pension scheme benefits   185
Table 8   Valuation interest rates   186
Table 9   Inflation and other financial assumptions   186
Table 10   Standard contribution rates under different tax
           regimes   187

Figure 1   Distribution of single pensioners' income, 2025   59
Figure 2   Distribution of single pensioners' income, 2050   60
Figure 3   Marginal tax rates for a single person with BSP
           of £60 per week – no housing benefit or council
           tax benefit   81

Figure 4   Marginal tax rates for a single person with
            BSP of £60 per week – paying rent of £200 per
            month and £600 in council tax   82
Figure 5   Difference between amount of state pensions
            and Pension Credit, by year of retirement
            (S2P capped)   83
Figure 6   Difference between amount of state pensions
            and Pension Credit, by year of retirement
            (S2P continues)   84
Figure 7   Assets required at retirement to exceed Pension
            Credit upper threshold by year of retirement   87
Figure 8   Interaction between Pension Credit and S2P   133
Figure 9   Marginal tax rates   170

The Way Out of the Pensions Quagmire

1 INTRODUCTION

Much of the writing on pensions over the past twenty years has concentrated on the issue of the unfunded burden of state pension provision. Economic work that has been intended to demonstrate the superiority of market provision has done so on the grounds that private, funded provision does not lead to the problem of a 'demographic time bomb' and implicit government debt in the same way that unfunded state provision can. The position of the UK, for example, has been compared favourably with that of many other EU countries. Writers on the other side of the debate have tried to demonstrate either that the demographic time bomb is not an important issue or that there is some kind of economic equivalence between funded and unfunded pensions. These issues are important but well researched by other authors.

There are other, equally important, microeconomic issues relating to the role of the state in pensions policy that, until recently, had not received the same attention as the problem of the unfunded pensions burden.[1] This monograph deals with such microeconomic issues. The authors come from two different perspectives. One is an economist confident that market solutions

---

1   This has changed. The recent Pickering review (Pickering, 2002) looked at simplifying the framework for pension provision, and recent work done by the Pensions Policy Institute, the Institute for Fiscal Studies and the Pensions Commission has also looked at microeconomic issues in pension provision.

to economic problems are superior to centrally planned solutions. The other is a practising actuary who believes that the state has an important role in pension provision. Nevertheless, despite the fact that the authors are not totally agreed on the potential solutions to the UK's pension problems, they do agree that the state could take a number of actions to reduce intervention in retirement income provision which would increase economic welfare and allow the market to work more effectively. The tax framework for pensions is incoherent;[2] the tax and benefits system works to create serious disincentives to save and work; the way in which the government chooses to supplement retirement incomes is far too complex; and regulation is both intrusive and ineffective at achieving what might be legitimate economic ends.

Reform must be radical

Many proposals to reform the state pension system have been put forward recently. These have often involved proposals to increase the basic state pension to reduce the impact of means-tested benefits or proposals for compulsory pension provision so that fewer people are likely to have to fall back on means-tested benefits. Such solutions might, or might not, improve slightly on the status quo. They entirely miss the point, however. The whole system of income provision in older age, in the UK, is incoherent from top to bottom. It encourages rent-seeking – the seeking of special privileges from the government – by particular groups that are very numerous in the electorate and by professionals and

---

2   The Finance Act 2004 has partly addressed some of the inconsistencies in the treatment of different products.

government employees who gain from making tax, regulatory and social security systems more complex. Indeed, the current system can be seen as a function of the process of rent-seeking. Free television licences, the tax-free lump sum from pension funds, special tax allowances for pensioners, the winter fuel allowance, increased means-tested benefits to help the poor and special taper rates to help those who suffered from increasing means-tested benefits can all be seen to have benefited one interest group or another to which a political party might find it convenient to appeal at an election. Almost every aspect of the state pension, benefit, regulation and tax system should be revisited and radically reformed.

There are so many different groups receiving special privileges under different parts of the current system that radical reform might lead to few net losers. People who lose from one reform may gain from another. This may make reform easier. For example, the extension of means testing has led to gains by groups who have saved little. But, on the other hand, the particular income tax system that pensioners face helps those with moderate savings. The system has grown as if politicians, having implemented a measure to benefit one group of people, have tried to implement a complementary measure to benefit the net losers from previous reforms. The result is incoherence, complexity and a quagmire. There is certainly the potential for huge net welfare gains from reform of the whole system.

Principles for pension reform

Our reform proposals, discussed in detail in Part 3, are based on a number of general principles.

1   There may be a legitimate role for the government in providing a single means-tested benefit in retirement to act as a safety net. There is no reason, however, for the characteristics and level of that benefit to differ from the characteristics and level of means-tested benefits before retirement. There may also be a role for the government in providing needs-contingent benefits (for example, cash payments to provide long-term care for the elderly). We do not discuss these further, however, as they should broadly be independent of the pensions system. Similarly, we do not discuss in detail the major non-cash, means-tested benefits, such as council tax and housing benefits, but there is a strong case for absorbing these into the single, basic means-tested benefit. The winter fuel allowance and free television licence should be abolished along with other, more minor, discretionary payments to pensioners.

2   The tax system for elderly people should be no different from that for younger people.

3   There is an economic case for the state to require a particular minimum level of compulsory pension provision because of the means-tested benefit safety net. But given our proposed reforms to means-tested benefits, this minimum compulsory level of pension provision need not be higher than it is currently. The fact that we have compulsory pension provision already is often totally ignored in the debate about compulsion. We should not have more compulsory pension provision than we currently do, although it should be differently designed. The state should provide a state pension at the minimum compulsory level, for those who have an appropriate national insurance contributions

record, although it should be permissible for people to make appropriate alternative provision by 'contracting out' of the whole of the state system.

4   Pension saving should remain outside the tax system until pension income is received – that is, tax relief should continue to be given on contributions to pension schemes. There should be no arbitrary benefits given to those who save for a pension, however. The tax-free lump sum should be abolished. On the other hand, arbitrary taxes such as the taxation of equity returns from equity dividends, begun in 1997, should be removed.

5   Given that pension saving should take place outside the tax system until benefits are received, it is reasonable for the Inland Revenue to place some limits on tax-relieved provision. These limits should simply be designed to prevent clear abuse, however. If the tax-free lump sum is removed, there are few possible abuses of the tax system and therefore no reason to have strict limits on pension provision given that these impose costs on savers and providers of products.

6   Regulation of the solvency and investment policy of pension schemes should be limited to those parts of schemes that are designed to provide the minimum required compulsory pension where people have decided to make private rather than state provision. Beyond that, regulation can become much less onerous and be limited to ensuring that schemes are operated transparently.

7   The pension system should not institutionalise a particular retirement age.

8   The level of compulsory minimum pension provision would form the basis for any annuitisation requirements.

Individuals would have to use pension funds to purchase annuities only in so far as is necessary to provide them with the compulsory minimum pension provision and ensure that they are not dependent on means-tested benefits.

The above principles would allow the pension system to operate in a free environment that should enable individuals and families to maximise their welfare. Currently the system of retirement income provision seems designed to maximise votes from interest groups. The above principles for reform focus the political and economic debate on the issue of how much income redistribution there should be through means-tested benefits and the degree of compulsory provision that is necessary to alleviate the moral hazard created by means-tested benefits. It is because these principles are enduring that any reforms based upon them would be enduring. The principles will adhere through changing demographic and financial conditions and proposals based on them will not become outdated as tax levels and systems change. Indeed, the proposals based on these principles are internationally applicable although, of course, the level of any compulsory minimum pension and the age from which it is paid may differ from country to country.

The above principles will also contribute considerably to the deinstitutionalisation of the retirement age. Premature part-time working and early retirement will no longer be artificially encouraged by special tax, pensions and benefit systems for those aged above 65 (or, in some cases, 60).

The proposals we have developed, based on these principles, are designed to discourage and as far as possible eliminate the rent-seeking that the current system encourages. Few other authors seem to have taken on board the important principles of public choice economics when looking at pensions policy options. Not to do so is a serious and fundamental error.

There is one further principle on which the authors are not agreed. One of the authors believes that the pension system should be reformed to maximise freedom of choice in pension provision, with funded provision, based on privately invested contributions, established as the norm for the provision of any compulsory minimum. The other author believes that there is a role for state retirement income provision (through the compulsory minimum). For the purposes of this monograph, we work on the basis that the state will provide a compulsory minimum level of retirement income but, as is noted above, any individual should be able to 'contract out' of the state system, with actuarially neutral national insurance rebates being paid, assuming that it can be demonstrated that appropriate private provision has been made.[3] Contracting out could be extended to those who do not pay national insurance contributions but still receive a pension entitlement from the state (for example, those receiving home responsibilities protection), although the authors disagree on how much of an advantage this would confer on savers.[4]

---

3   Again, one of the authors would prefer to have a 'tighter' definition of 'appropriate private provision' with some guarantee of the pension or the size of the fund that would be accumulated to buy the pension.

4   Seldon (1960), in one of the earliest IEA publications on pensions, opposed contracting out on a number of grounds. Many of those grounds are nullified, however, if (a) contracting-out rebates are actuarially neutral and related to the actuarial value of the benefit forgone and *not* to the individual's national insurance contributions, and (b) there is proper accounting for future state pension liabilities so that a person who contracts out would receive a cash payment but would also contribute towards an equivalent reduction in the government's pension liabilities which would be costed and on the government's balance sheet in a

A contributory pension not a citizen's pension

A number of proposals have been made for the development of a citizen's pension similar to the New Zealand model. The National Association of Pension Funds (NAPF) has set up a committee to look into its potential operation in the UK. The Pensions Policy Institute (PPI) has published favourable commentaries on the proposal (see O'Connell, 2004) and the NAPF has recently published a report, the research for which was undertaken by the PPI, examining how a citizen's pension could be achieved.[5]

In most of the proposals, a citizen's pension would be paid to anybody who passed a residency test, at a level that would be high enough to prevent a person from receiving means-tested benefits. It is quite possible that a citizen's pension, combined with the abolition of the state second pension (S2P), would lead to an improvement on the current situation. There are serious disadvantages with the approach, however, and its proponents seem to have ignored completely the influence of this type of system on the behaviour of large parts of the electorate. The citizen's pension would be set at an arbitrary level by the government of the day. At any time, pensioners, who are forming an increasing proportion of the electorate, could vote for its increase. Indeed, although less likely, the electorate could vote for its abolition! The pension would be even more politicised than it is today. A citizen's pension would provide an arbitrary redistribution of income, to be deter-

---

proper resource accounting system. With such a system, the government would not have the incentive that now exists to give rebates that are less than actuarially neutral.

5 See the interim report of the NAPF, produced by the PPI on 6 December 2004, at <http://www.pensionspolicyinstitute.org.uk/uploadeddocuments/NAPF_TCP_Interim_Report_Master_report_6Dec04.pdf>.

mined by the electorate of the day, from the working population to the pensioner population.

Some proposals have been made for an independent commission to fix the level of the pension. This is not credible. Given that the citizen's pension would be financed through taxes raised by Parliament, Parliament would have to have responsibility for setting its level. There is a potential role for an Independent Pensions Commission (see below and Part 3) but not one that sets the level of the pension.

Instead of a citizen's pension, we propose the maintenance of the contributory principle of pension provision. Indeed, we suggest making it more explicit in respect of the basic state benefit. The government would set the amount of pension (linked to an index, such as wages or prices) that would be accrued as a result of national insurance contributions in a given year. The cost of that pension would be borne quite explicitly by the generation that would receive it, through national insurance contributions, at the time of accrual, like the former State Earnings Related Pensions Scheme (SERPS) and its successor (S2P). There would be redistribution within the system because, for example, an earnings-related contribution might be paid to obtain a fixed benefit, but there would be no general incentive for those accruing a pension to vote for a higher rate of pension accrual – because there would be an increased national insurance cost in doing so. Of course, no parliament can bind its successor. Parliament could vote to increase or reduce pension entitlements after accrual. But this would be much more difficult than under a citizen's pension scheme because it would go against all the principles of the system. It has proved much more difficult, for example, for the government to tinker with *accrued* benefits in the SERPS and S2P systems that have an explicit accruals system, than it was for them to alter the up-rating of benefits in the basic state pension system. We also propose an Independent Pensions Commission (IPC) to take decisions that are essentially non-political and which relate to the protection of the value of accrued rights when changes are made to aspects of the state pension scheme.

As well as the political economy of the citizen's pension being highly problematic it is very difficult to see how contracting out of the state pension, if appropriate private provision were made, could be facilitated. Indeed, its proponents generally wish to end contracting out. This would be a retrograde step, removing choice and competition and requiring large numbers of people to rely on the state for much of their retirement income, even if they would prefer not to do so.

It is difficult to see a single advantage in the citizen's pension. Its proponents cite the advantage that it is received regardless of whether or not somebody has made contributions in their working lives. It is not obvious why this is an advantage. It is not difficult, under the accruals and contribution system that we propose, which has been the bedrock of pension provision (state and private) in the UK, to attribute notional contributions to particular groups of people who cannot make national insurance contributions (as is done for non-working parents with children up to a certain age and also for other groups in our current system). It is nevertheless true that in a pension system based on the contributory principle some people may 'slip through the net' and make insufficient contributions to receive a pension above means-tested benefit levels. Given the ease with which it is possible to obtain a contribution record for the basic state pension – and we propose using the same approach for our single state pension as is currently used for the basic state pension – the number of people who will be in receipt of the basic means-tested benefit will be relatively small. It does not seem reasonable to design a pension system that ensures that no individuals are in receipt of means-tested benefits after retirement any more than it seems reasonable to have a system whereby no individuals are in receipt of means-tested benefits before retirement.

The Turner Commission

When the Pensions Commission, chaired by Adair Turner, published its report in October 2004 it laid down a challenge to those involved in pensions policy. Four basic policy options were described by the commission: allowing pensioners to become relatively poorer; higher taxes or national insurance contributions; higher savings (including private pension provision); and higher average retirement ages.

The proposals in this monograph should certainly lead to a more soundly based state and private pension system and to greater voluntary labour force participation by those over 55.[6] They will also lead to much-reduced complexity, another problem identified by the Pensions Commission.

In the debate on pensions, little attention is given to the possibility of reducing the level of means-tested benefits. This is a fifth policy option, although one that could be regarded as implicit in the Pensions Commission's first option. In 1999, the proportion of

---

6   The phrase 'retirement ages must rise' used by the commission is not a helpful one as it gives the impression of retirement being a once-and-for-all decision. In a free labour market, participation in the labour force may still occur, even if people are not working full time.

pensioners in receipt of means-tested benefits was 37 per cent. The proportion had been falling for at least six years and would have continued to fall as the State Earnings Related Pension scheme matured. The Pensions Commission forecasts that, if current policies continue, 65 per cent of pensioners will be in receipt of means-tested benefits in retirement in 2050. The reason for this sea change is a rise in the level of means-tested benefits that took place from 1998 to 2003 and which is expected to continue. Most proposals for pension reform propose raising the state pension up to the new level of means-tested benefits. As stated above, our own proposals are that:

- Means-tested benefit levels should be the same pre and post age 65.
- The compulsory minimum pension requirement should be closely related to the means-tested benefit level so that anybody with a reasonably full contribution record will not receive means-tested benefits.
- It is a matter for Parliament to decide what level of means-tested benefits to offer at all ages.

In practice, this would imply either a reduction in means-tested minimum incomes paid to pensioners or an increase in those paid to people before age 65. This focuses the government's attention on what the basic safety net is that it wishes to provide and away from 'buying votes' by offering better minimum incomes to particular groups in the electorate. Of course, needs-based benefits could be provided to people in old age – whether they should be provided by the state or through private insurance is an entirely separate policy issue.

Microeconomic, not macroeconomic

We have not estimated the fiscal cost of proposed solutions. This is partly because the authors are sceptical of the accuracy of macroeconomic modelling, which is necessary to estimate such costs, and also because it is beyond the scope of our specialisations. Furthermore, we are more interested in looking at where policy changes could unambiguously enhance economic welfare by reducing the distortions created by current approaches: we believe that it is the role of the pensions economist to propose the design of *frameworks* for retirement income provision that meet certain economic criteria. Nevertheless, we have indicated where we believe that certain changes to the system would be fiscally neutral, not allowing for other welfare gains and behavioural changes. The fiscal cost of any proposal can be changed by changing the general level of tax allowances, the level of the compulsory minimum pension provision or the age from which the compulsory minimum is received, and by changing the level of the basic means-tested benefit.

The remainder of the monograph is organised as follows: Part 1 explains the current landscape of retirement income provision in the UK and identifies some of the problems; Part 2 analyses the problems that government policies have created in greater detail; Part 3 proposes solutions. The reader interested only in policy solutions could read Part 3 first and do so without any loss of continuity, as the framework we propose is not dependent on any particular starting point for current policy. Also, the framework we propose can be applied to other countries: again, the interested international reader could refer to Part 3, broadly ignoring the UK context.

Throughout we have used the phrase 'retirement income' to describe any form of income paid to somebody who has retired partially or fully or who has qualified for the receipt of income owing to their age. We use the phrase 'pension' to describe the payment of a life annuity, either from private sources or from the state, from a given age. We would like to make clear from the outset that one aspect of state intervention in retirement provision that we believe reduces economic welfare is the incentives that are created for individuals to retire at particular ages (or choose full rather than partial retirement). Thus, when we use the terms 'pension' and 'retirement income' we do not intend to convey the meaning of full income replacement from a pre-determined age.

There are two major issues that we do not discuss which are relevant to the pensions landscape. The first, as we have already mentioned, is the problem of non-cash means-tested benefits such as housing benefit and council tax benefit. These are a significant part of many pensioners' incomes but they raise a wider set of issues than those addressed here. The second is the extent of regulation of the selling process for personal pension products. Again, the regulation of the selling process raises a wider set of issues, although potentially important for people saving for pensions, across the whole of the financial sector.

Part 1
Wading Through the Quagmire

There are several main forms of retirement income in the UK. The most obvious are state pension provision and pension provision from private sector pension schemes. The latter can be either personal pensions or company pensions funded through occupational schemes. There are, however, a number of other forms of retirement income. Some of these originate from private savings and investment decisions (such as income from general savings or income from let properties). Others originate from government, such as means-tested benefits paid in retirement. Part 1 of this monograph analyses the sources of pensioner income today, as the background for the analysis of the shortcomings of the system and of policy proposals in later parts.

2 STATE RETIREMENT INCOME PROVISION

Benefits paid to a recipient purely on account of age (i.e. not related to another contingency such as disability) can be divided into three main categories: the basic state pension, earnings-related pensions and means-tested benefits, such as the Pension Credit. The third category can be further divided into cash benefits and benefits in kind (the latter including free television licences or housing benefit). A further category, benefits that are not means tested, are also paid to those of pension age (for example, winter fuel allowance). In the remainder of this chapter we explain the current pattern of income provided by the state for those of retirement age.

Basic state pension

The basic state pension is paid to all who have an appropriate contribution record. It is contributory, not means tested, and its level does not depend on the earnings of an individual at retirement. The contribution record is gained by making compulsory national insurance (NI) contributions in employment, although a record will also be given to those who undertake caring responsibilities in the home, such as looking after children. The total contribution is dependent on earnings up to the Upper Earnings Limit,[1] while the pension is

---

1   Although this position is further complicated by the fact that there is no upper

a fixed amount. The link between contributions and the pension paid is therefore an imperfect one, and this system of providing state pensions is often said to redistribute income towards the poor. Such income redistribution is ambiguous, however, for two reasons. Those on low incomes are likely to enter the workforce at an earlier age and could have more years of contributions (up to 49 years, which is five years longer than the maximum period for which an individual has to work to qualify for a full pension). Second, those on low incomes are likely to receive the pension for a shorter time period (and, indeed, are less likely to receive a pension at all) because their mortality is higher.

From April 2004, the basic state pension was paid at the rate of £79.60 per week for single people and £127.25 per week for couples. It is paid from age 65 (although women will continue to retire earlier than this until 2020 and can obtain a full pension with fewer years of contributions). Eighty-five per cent of men and 49 per cent of women have contribution records that qualify them for the full basic state pension. Since 1980, the basic state pension has been indexed to increases in the general level of prices, as measured by the increase in the Retail Price Index. The current government has pledged that annual increases will not be less than 2.5 per cent. Until 1978 women could opt to pay a lower national insurance rate and not accrue basic state pension rights. This option was then withdrawn for new entrants into the system. Also in 1978, 'Home Responsibilities Protection' was introduced. This effectively enables carers to receive national insurance contribution credits (for example, if they are receiving child benefit).

---

earnings limit for employers and it has been removed in respect of a 1 per cent employee's national insurance contribution.

These two measures will continue to increase the proportion of women with a full contribution record in the coming years.

Second state pension

The second tier of the UK state system is the State Second Pension (S2P), formerly the State Earnings Related Pension Scheme (SERPS). We will describe SERPS first, as this system (although not straightforward) was easier to understand than its successor. We will then explain how S2P differs from SERPS.

SERPS was, and S2P remains, a contributory defined benefit (DB) scheme, with contributions being made through the national insurance system, as for the basic state pension. The benefit is based on the revalued career average principle. Under the accrual rules for SERPS, in each year in which a person pays national insurance contributions (NICs), earnings between the lower earnings limit (£4,108 p.a. in 2004/5) and the upper earnings limit (£31,720 p.a. in 2004/5) are revalued in line with national average earnings up to retirement. The total of such revalued earnings is multiplied by an age-dependent fraction[2] for every year of NICs paid. The fraction is chosen so that the maximum SERPS pension, earned after a full working history of 49 years, represents 20 per cent of a person's revalued 'relevant' earnings.[3] Once the pension starts payment, it is linked to prices rather than earnings.

---

2 Accrual is age dependent because full entitlement to SERPS was accelerated for those aged over sixteen when it was first introduced. For those reaching state pension age after 2027 the rate of accrual per year is 0.2/49.

3 Between 1978, when SERPS was first introduced, and 1988 the target pension was 25 per cent of relevant earnings and the accrual rules favoured people with broken career histories.

Provision of pension up to the level of SERPS/S2P is compulsory for employed people. Membership of SERPS/S2P itself, however, is effectively voluntary as individuals can 'contract out' either by joining a contracted-out occupational scheme or by taking out an appropriate personal pension (APP). Occupational schemes can contract out on a defined benefit or a defined contribution basis, in which case the employer and employee pay lower NICs. Occupational schemes that are contracted out on a defined benefit basis have to provide a minimum level of benefit. If they contract out on a defined contribution basis, a 'minimum contribution', equal to the difference between the full and the lower contracted-out rate of NICs, must be paid by the employer to the member's fund, and the government pays an age-related rebate of NICs to the member's fund also. If individuals contract out through an APP both employer and employee pay full NICs but a rebate (also age related) is paid directly by the government to the member's APP. There are regulations that govern how the fund accumulated from the NI rebates can be used when members retire. These regulations are partly designed to protect the social security system from moral hazard (for example, they require the purchase of particular forms of annuity).

The national insurance rebates are intended to reflect the value of the loss of the SERPS/S2P benefit for those contracting out. Under the SERPS system they generally did so; we will comment further on the rebates under S2P below. In defined contribution (DC) contracted-out schemes, the age-related invested NIC rebate would accumulate, on the basis of reasonable assumptions for expected investment returns, to provide the individual with a pension broadly equivalent to the SERPS benefit. The Government Actuary reviews the rebates every five years. The last review took place in 2000/1, for implementation from April 2002.

The government has made changes to the state pension system and the impact of these changes will evolve gradually over the coming years. The rationale and the underlying principles are laid out in the government Green Paper *A New Contract for Welfare: Partnership in Pensions* (DSS, 1998).

Since April 2002 SERPS has been replaced by the 'State Second Pension' (S2P). It is not possible to explain the S2P system in 'educated lay person's terms'. We ask the reader to bear with the authors until the end of this section, which is necessarily complex.

SERPS accrual rates were the same at all levels of pay between the lower and upper earnings limits, and prior to April 2002 contracted-out rebates varied only by age and by contracting-out vehicle.[4] Under S2P the accrual rate varies since the state 'earnings related' target pension is:

- 40 per cent (twice the SERPS target) for earnings between the Lower Earnings Limit (LEL) and the Lower Earnings Threshold (£11,600 in 2004/5), with those earning less than the Lower Earnings Threshold being treated as though their earnings equalled the Lower Earnings Threshold (LET);
- 10 per cent (half the SERPS target) on earnings between the LET and an upper limit colloquially known as the Upper Earnings Threshold (calculated as $3 \times LET - 2 \times LEL$, which will be £26,600 in 2004/5);

---

4   Differences in age-related rebates between occupational DC schemes and APPs are explained by differences in expenses and the timing of payments. In contracted-out DB schemes the 'rebate' is not age related.

- 20 per cent (the same as the SERPS target) on earnings between the Upper Earnings Threshold and the Upper Earnings Limit.

Effectively, S2P targets a flat-rate pension (£2,997 p.a. in 2004/5 for someone with a full working lifetime) on earnings up to the Lower Earnings Threshold; those earning less than the Upper Earnings Threshold will receive a higher pension than they would have received under SERPS; those earning more than the Upper Earnings Threshold will receive the same pension as they would have received under SERPS.

Contracted-out rebates will continue to be based on earnings and the amount of the rebate will depend on the nature of the contracted-out pension scheme. If the scheme is an APP then the rebates will also reflect the different accrual rates. Members of APP schemes earning less than the Lower Earnings Threshold will receive an S2P 'top-up' to reflect the difference between their accrual (based on the Lower Earnings Threshold) and the rebate (based on their actual earnings). The rebates paid in respect of members of contracted-out occupational schemes are based on a 20 per cent accrual rate only. Consequently, members earning less than the Upper Earnings Threshold will also receive an S2P 'top-up', although this 'top-up' might be very small for a large number of individuals.

It was originally proposed that, from 2006/7, the earnings-related part of the S2P would stop and it would become flat rate only. This proposition was subject to stakeholder pension schemes becoming successful and the government has not indicated whether or not this is still to go ahead. The intention is, however, that contracted-out rebates will continue to be earnings related. If this were to happen it would introduce new incentives to contract out of S2P for people paid more than the LET, complicating individuals' decisions to contract out of the S2P and making it more difficult to make long-term rational decisions: see Part 2.

There are two main objectives of the change from SERPS to S2P. It will create an extra state pension entitlement above the basic state pension for those on very low earnings (including those with certain caring responsibilities). Second, it may increase the level of state pension (or state pension combined with private pension purchased with S2P rebates for those who contract out) for anybody earning up to the Upper Earnings Threshold.

Proposals for the introduction of stakeholder pensions were also made in the Green Paper. These proposals were enacted in the Welfare Reform Act (1999). They involve the development of new private pension vehicles on a defined contribution basis and will be discussed in the section on private provision.

In principle, defined benefit pension schemes are not especially complex and SERPS was reasonably comprehensible. The S2P system is a good example of how the state pension system has been manipulated to achieve political goals – which may or may not be worthy in themselves – leaving us with a system that is virtually incomprehensible.

Aspects of the political economy of the contracting-out system

In terms of political economy, the system of contracting out of S2P is a very interesting one. Much has been written in 'public choice economics'[5] about the behaviour of 'rent-seeking groups'. In a democratic state, organised interest groups have much to gain from electing politicians who will distribute sums of money (or goods and services provided through the political system) to those groups. Such rent-seeking groups often receive significant benefits from politicians in these circumstances. The criteria that make rent-seeking groups successful include a requirement for the costs of such government action to be relatively dispersed among large groups of voters but the benefits to be relatively concentrated among a smaller number of voters who then have a strong incentive to invest time and money campaigning for the reallocation of resources.[6] The UK S2P system makes such behaviour less productive for interest groups, as did the much less complex SERPS system. The benefit is defined on entry into the system and members have to pay for those benefits through contributions. Thus if the electorate vote themselves higher rates of pension accrual in the system, they are also voting themselves higher rates of national insurance contributions. Second, any individual can opt out of the benefit on terms intended to be actuarially neutral. There is, in effect, no government subsidy for those in the system because anybody who chooses to leave the system will be entitled to a rebate of taxes (in the form of NICs) notionally equal to the value of the benefit forgone.[7] The contribution principle of S2P and the contracting-out system are the redeeming features of the UK pension system which it is worthwhile retaining.

5   See, for example, Tullock et al. (2000).
6   See also Friedman and Friedman (1985), who provide a good discussion of these issues.
7   There has been controversy over the size of the rebates, however, first in 1997 after the increase in tax on pension funds equity holdings and more recently after the 2001 review of rebate levels.

More generally, the contracting-out system is an unusual but seemingly effective method of putting the claims of those who prefer state provision to the market test – indeed, it is also an effective way of putting the claims of those who prefer market provision to the test. Most provision of services by the state involves either a state monopoly or state licensing of a limited number of providers (for example, letter delivery and the provision of television services), or else the state provides the service free of charge at the point of delivery, such as in health and education (a citizen's pension would also have this characteristic). In these cases, those who use a private service have to pay taxes for the provision of the state service as well as for the cost of the private service. The SERPS contracting-out system, however, is similar to a voucher system (see, for example, Friedman and Friedman, 1980, for an interesting and lucid discussion of vouchers in education): it allows individuals to choose between the state service and a range of alternative private providers.

The state can still pursue objectives of imposing the provision of 'merit goods' under the contracting-out system. If it is felt that individuals systematically underestimate the amount of pension provision they need to make, the government may regard it as desirable to impose a certain degree of pension provision. The recognition that pensions may have merit good qualities or externalities attached to them leads many to the conclusion that there should be compulsory pension provision, just as there is compulsory provision of education. The extent of compulsory pension provision in the UK is defined by the basic state pension (from which individuals cannot contract out) plus S2P. We discuss whether there should be more compulsory provision in Part 3.

Means-tested social security benefits in retirement

The second form of state retirement income provision is means-tested benefits paid in retirement. There are two categories: cash benefits, such as income support or Pension Credit (which incorporates the minimum income guarantee [MIG])[8], and benefits in kind or non-cash benefits such as housing benefit. Where non-cash benefits are paid, the average level of such non-cash benefits is over £65 per week. Different tapers apply to different benefits (see below). All means-tested benefits are determined by the level of household income and/or assets, rather than being individualised.

The MIG should ensure that no pensioner aged over 60 (the current state pension age for women) has an income of less than £105.45 per week (£160.95 per week for a couple) from April 2004. These amounts are greater than the Basic State Pension (BSP), so individuals whose only retirement income is the BSP will also receive MIG.

In October 2003 the Pension Credit system subsumed the MIG, although only pensioners aged over 65 will be eligible for the 'savings credit' element of pension credit. The savings credit is designed so that the marginal withdrawal rate of benefit will be pound for pound on private income received up to the level of BSP and then 40 pence in the pound for any private income received over the level of the BSP. Thus every extra pound of private income earned over the BSP leads to a 40 pence reduction in the level of benefits received. This new Pension Credit system reduces the withdrawal rate of benefit by 60 pence for every pound of

---

8   The MIG is now called the 'guarantee credit', but we will continue to refer to the MIG – a more descriptive name.

private income earned above the BSP, as compared with the MIG regime, but creates a much wider band of income over which benefit is withdrawn. The overall impact, however, is complicated much further by the interaction of the pension credit with non-cash, means-tested benefits and the different treatment of couples and single people, as well as the impact of the tax system. Pension Credit is discussed further in Clark (2001), and we undertake our own analysis in Part 2.

Entitlement to means-tested benefits also depends on assets or capital accumulated. Savings are deemed to yield a weekly income of £1 for each £500 in excess of £6,000, which is added to other private income for the purpose of calculating means-tested benefits.

Non-cash means tested benefits in retirement

A considerable proportion of means-tested benefits is paid in 'non-cash' form. The major non-cash benefits are council tax benefit and housing benefit. Full council tax and rent are rebated for all those who have income up to the MIG. The capital qualifications are different from those relating to MIG and Pension Credit. An individual who has capital of more than £16,000 does not receive housing or council tax benefit. Those eligible for the MIG lose 65 pence of housing benefit and 20 pence of council tax benefit for each £1 of income above that threshold. If they are also eligible for savings credit, then the marginal tax rate experienced is 91 per cent. This further extends the reach of means testing, with high levels of benefit withdrawal at incomes significantly above the Pension Credit limit.

There are other difficulties with housing benefit. For older people, it is not needs based. This means that pensioners receive the full level of benefit for living in houses that are bigger than their needs: there is no incentive for them to reduce their housing use unless the marginal value of extra space to the occupier is zero.

Non-means-tested social security benefits in retirement

In recent years, non-means-tested social security benefits have been introduced for individuals and households of pensionable age. There is a winter fuel allowance of £200 (rising to £350 at age 80). This should be regarded as a cash benefit, rather than a non-cash benefit, because it is paid at the same rate, regardless of the amount of winter fuel consumed. To qualify, an individual must be aged 60 or over and resident in the UK. A free television licence is given to any household that has a member over the age of 75. This is a non-cash, non-means-tested social security benefit: it would not be paid to somebody who did not own a television.

Total government spending on income provision in old age

Total government spending on income provision in old age is of the order of £75 billion per year, although the classification of some of this spending can be disputed. The government suggested in its 1997 Green Paper that total spending would increase by £0.5 billion per year in the short term and £5 billion per year in the long term as a result of reforms proposed in the Green Paper and now enacted. The long-term effects are particularly hard to estimate, however, because of the possible impact of increased means-tested benefit provision and the impact of other measures (such as the withdrawal of tax benefits from pension funds in the July 1997 Budget) on private pension provision. If these policies reduce private pension provision, state expenditure on means-tested benefits may increase more than expected.

Government statistics show the following payments made to pensioners in the fiscal year 2002/3:

Type of Benefit	Expenditure
SERPS rebates[1]	£ 11.1 bn
Payments of basic state pension[2]	£ 38.4 bn
Payments of SERPS pensions[2]	£ 6.1 bn
Payments of non-income-related benefits[2]	£10.8 bn
Payments of income-related benefits[2]	£10.9 bn

1 Source: Report by the Government Actuary on the Drafts of the Social Security Benefits Uprating Order 2003 and the Social Security (Contributions) (Re-rating and National Insurance Funds Payments) Order 2003, <http://www.gad.gov.uk/publications/docs/2003uprating.pdf>

2 Source: DWP Benefit Expenditure tables, 2003, <http://www.dwp.gov.uk/asd/asd4/Table5.xls>

SERPS rebates are rebates of national insurance contributions for people who had contracted out of SERPS. They are essentially a return of NICs rather than a form of government spending, as explained earlier.

3 PRIVATE RETIREMENT INCOME PROVISION

Occupational pension provision

Occupational pension provision is undergoing substantial changes, but it is still the case that the largest schemes are defined benefit, providing a pension based on salary at or close to retirement and depending on the number of years' membership of the scheme. The most common accrual rate in defined benefit pension schemes in the private sector is 1/60ths. In the public sector 1/80ths is more common, but members accrue a lump-sum benefit in addition to their pension, so that the overall rates of accrual are similar.

There is no obligation on employers to establish occupational pension schemes and, when they do establish schemes, membership cannot be made a condition of employment.[1] Schemes are usually set up under Trust Law and have benefit and contribution arrangements that comply with the Income and Corporation Taxes Act 1988, so that contributions are made out of pre-tax income and investment returns are not subject to tax in the hands of the

---

1   Membership of an occupational scheme could be made a condition of employment until 1987, when compulsory membership was prohibited under the 1986 Social Security Act. A recent Green Paper considered whether employers should be given this right once again (DWP, 2002), but there are no firm plans to revive the right.

pension fund, although, as is discussed in Part 2, no tax reclaim can now be made in respect of taxed income from equity investments. While the employer is responsible for the scheme's establishment and pays (directly or indirectly) towards the benefits it provides, scheme trustees are responsible for its management.

Under Trust Law, trustees are obliged to act in the best interests of the members of the scheme. The 1995 Pension Act codified some of the obligations of trustees with particular regard to occupational schemes, including trustees' responsibilities as investors of the scheme's assets and their responsibility for ensuring the proper funding of the scheme. It also restricted who can be a trustee. The Pensions Act 2004 has extended some of these codifications of trustees' duties.

The level of regulation and control of benefits imposed on occupational schemes has increased significantly since 1978, when schemes were first permitted to contract out of SERPS. This has led to a move away from defined benefit (DB) towards defined contribution (DC) occupational provision, although there are also other reasons for this trend. In the past five years the majority of new occupational pension schemes have been DC, while many DB schemes have been closed. Based on the experience of companies in the FTSE 350, the number of companies with open DB schemes (not necessarily open to all employee groups) had fallen to 40 per cent by the end of 2003 (from research by Mercer HR Consulting available at <www.mercerhr.com>).

Usually employees are expected to contribute about 5 per cent of pay to a DB occupational scheme while the employer meets the 'balance of the cost'. This means that, in theory, the employer has an open-ended commitment to the scheme. The financially significant risks are from lower than expected investment returns and increased longevity, and employers might be expected to make additional contributions to meet any shortfall in assets relative to liabilities. To a certain extent the employer can control this cost either by limiting salary growth or, *in extremis*, by closing the scheme. Since June 2003, however, solvent employers have been obliged to pay to buy out defined benefit liabilities if they wind up a scheme, making it unlikely that many employers would pursue this course lightly. On average, in 2002, employers contributed about 12 per cent of pay to DB schemes.[2]

In a DC scheme the member effectively meets the balance of the cost, since the employer pays a fixed contribution and the member takes the risk that investment performance will be lower than anticipated. The average contribution rates to occupational DC schemes are 5 per cent by the employee and 6 per cent by the employer.[3]

Although occupational DC schemes are established under trust and share some of the regulations of DB schemes, since they do not raise the expectation of a guaranteed level of benefit at retirement the regulations that apply are much lighter. Employers replacing a DB with a DC scheme save on the expense and risk of running a DB scheme, and at the same time have taken the opportunity to cut employee benefits (while, arguably, making the employee benefit package more transparent).

DC schemes do not provide good benefits upon death before retirement, since the accumulated fund at the time of death will generally be small relative to need at that time. The majority of schemes, however, provide insurance benefits along-

---

2   NAPF (2002).
3   Ibid.

side the occupational scheme, which can compensate for this shortcoming.

Occupational schemes must give members the opportunity to pay additional voluntary contributions (AVCs) into an investment facility provided by the scheme in order to enhance their pension.

Stakeholder and personal pensions

Individuals who are self-employed, choose not to participate in a company arrangement or work for a company without a company pension arrangement may save for their retirement in a personal pension plan. A personal pension is a savings vehicle that qualifies for special tax treatment (again, see Part 2 for a full discussion of the tax treatment). In return for this special tax treatment, certain conditions have to be met relating to contribution limits and the form in which benefits can be taken. It is intended that benefits are taken as an annuity, although 25 per cent of the fund can be taken as a tax-free lump sum and limited income drawdown[4] is permitted. In principle, personal pension plans and defined contribution company pension schemes are very similar, although there are many practical differences (see Part 2).

Stakeholder plans, which are a special category of personal pension plan, were introduced by the Welfare Reform and Pensions Act 1999 and have been available since April 2001. Stakeholder plans are more heavily regulated than personal pensions. In particular, they must have:

---

4   Income drawdown occurs where the fund is not used to buy an annuity upon retirement but income is taken from the fund which otherwise remains invested.

1   a maximum level of charge;
2   a low minimum contribution;
3   freedom to stop and start contributions without penalty;
4   freedom to transfer the fund to another company without penalty; and
5   minimum levels of disclosure.

From October 2001, employers with five or more 'relevant'[5] employees must provide access to a stakeholder scheme and administer payroll deduction to the scheme if requested by an employee. The government hopes that they will form a cheaper vehicle than standard personal pensions so that those in low-to-middle income groups will be encouraged to save in them.

It remains to be seen whether stakeholder pensions will lead to an increase in private pension saving among low-to-middle income earners: there are a number of potential impediments to this discussed in Part 2. Between April 2001 and August 2003 about 1.25 million stakeholder pensions had been sold. About a third of these, however, are in respect of transfers from other pension arrangements and the monthly rate of sales has fallen (ABI, 2003). It is also difficult to determine how many of the stakeholder plans have been sold to 'non-target groups' such as children or spouses of individuals with a high income, although the ABI analysis estimates that only 3 per cent were provided for those not of working age.

More generally, reliable data on the number of employees and self-employed in each type of private pension scheme is

---

5   'Relevant' employees are, very broadly, all employees who have worked for their employer for more than three months and do not have access to an occupational pension scheme or personal pension scheme to which the employer contributes.

Table 1 **Current pension scheme membership by age and sex (percentages)**

	Employed	Self-employed
Men full time		
Occupational pension	55	
Personal pension	19	64
Any pension	66	
Women full time		
Occupational pension	60	
Personal pension	12	54
Any pension	66	
Women part time		
Occupational pension	33	
Personal pension	9	38
Any pension	39	

1 The percentages holding some type of pension do not sum to the percentage holding any pension because some people will hold more than one type of pension.
2 Self-employed percentages include people who have had a personal pension plan but are not currently contributing to it.
3 Self-employed men include both full- and part-time workers.
Source: ONS, 2004

not readily available. There tends to be a great deal of double counting, since some individuals have been members of a number of schemes. For example, someone could be a member of more than one personal pension scheme and also have a deferred occupational pension. In addition, an individual can be a member of an occupational scheme while making AVCs to provide extra income on retirement. According to GAD (2003), however, 10.1 million people in the UK are active members of occupational schemes (this would include defined benefit and defined contribution schemes) and about 10 million personal pensions are held (but this would include some double counting). Table 1 shows the proportion of people in different groups who have some pension saving.

The market value of all self-administered pension fund assets is approximately £550 billion.[6] This, however, excludes personal pension fund assets (which are classified in official statistics as part of the assets of other financial institutions such as insurance companies). The recent history of government statistics relating to occupational pension provision makes it difficult to be confident about the current value of funds and recent trends in their growth.

---

6   Estimate, as at December 2003, provided by Mercer HR Consulting Limited, based on FRS17 disclosures for FTSE350 companies.

4 SOURCES OF RETIREMENT INCOME

State benefits provide most of the income in retirement for large numbers of people, but it is possible for an individual to be in receipt of income from all the sources discussed in Chapters 2 and 3. Table 2 shows the actual and projected distribution of income between sources for a single pensioner on 'median' income in 2000, 2025 and 2050.

The figures for 2000 and 2025 are taken from Kumar and Ward (1999). The estimates for 2050 were extrapolated from those figures using the Government Actuary's population projections and are updated from similar projections published in Booth, Cooper and Stein (2000) to allow for the introduction of S2P and the Pension Credit.

There are four significant changes in the distribution of provision over time. These arise from:

1 the fall in the value of the basic state pension relative to earnings;
2 the replacement of SERPS by S2P;
3 the assumed increase in income from personal, or stakeholder, pension plans;
4 an increase in the amount of means-tested benefits provided.

The income distribution projected by Kumar and Ward,

Table 2 **Individual on median income: sources of retirement income**

	2000	*2025*	*2050*
Basic state pension	53.4%	39.3%	21.5%
S2P/SERPS/GRB	9.2%	24.8%	21.6%
Occupational pensions	9.3%	9.9%	7.8%
Investment income/personal pension/ stakeholder pension	5.1%	9.6%	21.0%
Earnings and other income	0.5%	0.1%	0.1%
Income support and housing benefit	22.5%	16.3%	28.0%
Total income (£ per week)	105.60	143.70	263.10

which was produced by a model called PENSIM, estimates that the proportion of income provided by the state will fall between 2000 and 2025. Our estimates[1] imply that the likely effect of the changes to state pensions and the introduction of the Pension Credit will be to reverse this trend in the very long term.

Differences in income sources across the income distribution

Figures in the Pensions Commission report published in October 2004 suggest that 64 per cent of pensioner incomes came from the state in 2002 (57 per cent if government occupational schemes are classed as private sources). This is not inconsistent with the position of the person on median income above because the income of the person on median income is less than the mean level of income and state provision is concentrated in lower income groups.

More detailed cross-sectional data, grouping the population

---

1   Calculated by projecting forward the PENSIM estimates allowing for S2P and Pension Credit and assuming that benefit structures, rates of inflation and earnings growth, and levels of uptake of means-tested benefits, remain the same.

Figure 1   **Distribution of single pensioners' incomes, 2025**

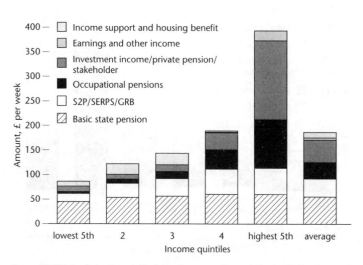

Source: *PENSIM, Developing Dynamic Simulation*, Government Economic Service Working Paper no. 136, 1999

by quintile, shows a picture where private pension provision is concentrated in particular groups whereas state retirement income provision (of various types) is the major source of income for those on low earnings.

The projected income distribution by quintile for 2025 and 2050 is shown in Figures 1 and 2. These charts also show the different sources of income for different groups within the income distribution spectrum.

This analysis is important because it is a government objective to increase the reliance on private retirement income sources for those in the lower quintiles. In *A New Contract for Welfare* (DSS,

Figure 2   **Distribution of single pensioners' incomes, 2050**

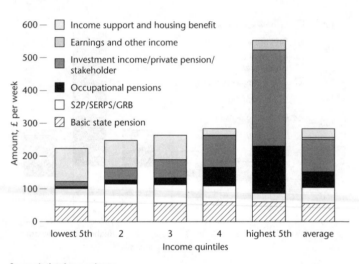

Source: Authors' own estimates

1998), the government states that it wants to shift the share of pension provision from the current ratios of 40 per cent private and 60 per cent state to 60 per cent private and 40 per cent state. This was one of the main objectives of the major changes to the pensions and welfare systems that resulted from the Green Paper. Table 2, together with the analysis of incentives for private retirement income provision in Part 2, shows that this is unlikely to be achieved. In so far as there is a movement in the direction that the government has stated it would prefer, it will probably bypass those in lower income groups. As we shall see later, any individual on moderate earnings without access to an occupational scheme is unlikely to have an incentive to make private retirement income provision. Figures 1 and 2 confirm that, even on conservative assumptions, there is projected to be a considerable increase in means-tested benefits for the second and third quintiles (the government's target group for the new stakeholder pensions).

Specifically, it can be seen from Figures 1 and 2 that retirement income provision is likely to continue to be predominantly from the state for all but the top 20 per cent of the income distribution, with the next 20 per cent receiving a considerable proportion from both state and private sources. There is certainly no sign of the reversing of the proportions of private and state income provision that the government seeks. This is not surprising given that means-tested benefit systems have now been developed which pay benefits to over half the retired population, a proportion that will rise to two-thirds on most projections.

5 COMPARISON WITH RETIREMENT INCOME PROVISION OVERSEAS

A brief analysis of international pension provision will be useful in providing background and context for the UK position. The starting point for analysis of pensions systems is often the 'pillar breakdown'. Hagemann and Nicoletti (1989) divide pension provision into three tiers or 'pillars'. Pillar one is state provision financed using a pay-as-you-go system. Pillar two is compulsory private provision. Pillar three is voluntary pensions saving above and beyond pillar two.

The major difference between the UK system and that in most of continental Europe is the extent of pillar one provision, which in the UK is limited to the basic state pension, set below subsistence levels and augmented by means-tested benefits. SERPS/S2P, although provided by the state, is probably better described as pillar two provision as it defines the minimum required private provision for individuals who contract out.[1] Pillar two is limited to the benefit from accumulating the contracted-out rebate or the minimum benefits that have to be provided if contracting out is on a defined benefit basis.

The different pillars need not be completely separate. Workers who are members of a contracted-out defined benefit occupational

---

1 Although because national insurance rebates are now significantly less than the actuarial value of the S2P given up as a result of contracting out, it is likely that there will be a gradual erosion of the contracting-out principle.

scheme, for example, are likely to be receiving benefit levels within that scheme which combine the compulsory minimum pillar two provision with voluntary pillar three provision.

One measure of the extent of pension provision is the 'replacement rate', which measures pension benefits as a percentage of final wages. Kenc and Perraudin (1997) produced some comprehensive work on the replacement ratio and the different forms state pensions systems took in different EU countries, but here we use figures from O'Connell (2003) and Daykin (2002) which are more up to date.

In Ireland, Australia, New Zealand and the UK, spending on state pensions is less than 5 per cent of GDP, and the replacement rate of the state pension is between 25 and 35 per cent (it is approximately in the middle of the range for the UK). The USA, the Netherlands, Denmark and Sweden provide a replacement rate of between 40 and 50 per cent and all spend between 5 and 10 per cent of GDP on state pensions – except the USA, which spends less than 5 per cent. Spain, Germany, France and Italy provide a replacement rate of between 65 and 75 per cent and spend 10 per cent or more of GDP providing state pensions. The replacement rate of total income (private income, state pension and state means-tested benefits) for those over age 65, in the UK, is 78 per cent, which is approximately average for OECD countries. This reflects the greater private provision in the UK but also greater non-pension, means-tested benefits. S2P will increase the replacement rate provided by the state for low earners, particularly those paid less than the Lower Earnings Threshold, although the contribution of the BSP will steadily decline as this is linked to prices.

State pensions are not generally pre-funded, in that a separate fund of investments is not held to meet future obligations. The level of unfunded pension debts will depend on a number of factors other than the replacement rate – for example, the demographic profile of the population; the terms on which a pension is received; the age from which a pension is received; and the 'generosity' of early retirement benefits. There are great differences between OECD countries in each of these respects. For example, each of Germany, France, the Netherlands, Spain and Sweden has indexation of pensions to average wages post retirement – in the UK, indexation is to prices, even for S2P; France has a retirement age of 60 as well as extremely 'generous' early retirement provision (thus lowering the effective age from which it is possible to receive a state pension). One illustration of the different demographic profiles is that, in Spain, the proportion of people over 65 is 50 per cent greater than in Ireland.

Private pension arrangements also vary between countries. Arrangements in the EU are discussed in Daykin (1998, 2002). They are often known as 'complementary provision' because they tend to supplement rather than replace state provision. In Germany, it is common for private pension schemes to be financed through 'book reserves'. Instead of independent funds being set up, which is the norm in the UK, employers promise to pay future pensions and make provision for those pensions on their balance sheets. This can provide less security because, if the employer becomes insolvent, any assets set aside for pension provision may be lost as well. Consequently, part of the benefit has to be insured.

In France, there is compulsory membership of industry-based 'pay-as-you-go' schemes. The pensions for today's pensioners are financed from the contributions of today's active members, rather than from the investment of previous contributions. Throughout

Europe there is a diversity of systems and institutional arrangements. Reform of pension systems in many EU countries is taking place. Attempts are being made to limit pensions, raise retirement ages and, in particular, reduce early retirement incentives. Reform is not, however, changing the landscape dramatically.

Systems also vary outside continental Europe, but many of the more recently reformed systems rely on defined contribution, privately funded schemes with a minimum compulsory contribution. The Australian system, for example, has a 'quasi-compulsory' minimum employee contribution towards a superannuation scheme of 9 per cent. Only 17 per cent of employees are members of defined benefit schemes. Most of the rest belong to defined contribution schemes. Schemes are often run on an industry-wide basis with trade union and employer trustees. There is a strong incentive to take a lump-sum retirement benefit (which can be up to 100 per cent of total benefits) and thus maximise means-tested benefits from the state later in retirement (Knox, 1998).

Many individuals in the USA hold 'individual retirement accounts' or 401(k) plans, which are defined contribution pension accounts that allow deferral of income tax. By the end of 2002 some estimates set 401(k) balances as high as $2.4 trillion (Hewitt Associates survey, *Hot topics in 401(k) plans*, 2002). Employer contributions to 401(k) plans are often made to match or supplement employee contributions. Employers' contributions can be made in the form of its shares, which can result in the exposure of significant pension savings to the fortunes of the employee's company. Withdrawals from 401(k) plans can be made at any time, although there may be a tax charge if the funds are not rolled over into another retirement plan.

The US social security retirement plan (known as OASI – old-age and survivors' insurance) has its origins in the Social Security Act of 1935. Major reform of the system was undertaken in 1983 (see Diamond and Gruber in Gruber and Wise, 1999). The reforms included a phased increase in the retirement age to 67, which will apply in the 2020s. Various reforms increased benefits significantly in the 1970s (often this was unintended, for example as a result of the over-indexation of benefits). Flexibility is allowed in that individuals can retire on increased benefits after the normal retirement age or on reduced benefits before the normal retirement age. Taxation of a proportion of social security benefits was also introduced.

Social security pensions are financed from a payroll tax, which is levied on earnings. The retirement pension is determined by earnings in the qualifying period, which are up-rated according to national average earnings. Total revalued qualifying earnings are then multiplied by scaling factors determined in such a way that the replacement ratio of pension to final salary is likely to fall significantly as income rises: a form of means testing. Replacement ratios fall from around 50 per cent for low income earners to 24 per cent for those who earn the maximum salary on which social security taxes are paid throughout working life. There is considerable income redistribution within the system. Given Bush's re-election it seems likely that a form of 'contracting out' will be developed whereby part of an employee's social security contributions will be diverted to private retirement saving schemes.

The Chilean system, described in Pinera (1998), has provided a model for a number of other countries in South and Central America, as well as in Central and Eastern Europe. Reforms to the Polish system that have some of the characteristics of the Chilean system, for example, are discussed in Stroinski (1998). Chile had had a state pension system since 1925, but by the late 1970s the contribution rate had risen to 20 per cent of total payroll, despite a low level of benefits. The Chilean system was then reformed in 1980. Schemes are privately run, but follow a state blueprint that includes a high level of regulation. Employees have to contribute a minimum of 10 per cent of earnings up to the first $22,000 of earnings. There are then tax incentives to contribute up to a further 10 per cent of earnings. The contributions are paid to a defined contribution plan. The state guarantees a particular minimum pension and, if the accumulated fund does not buy a sufficient annuity at retirement, it is 'topped up' by the government. Chilean private pension funds now total 30 per cent of national income.

The countries that have adopted a Chilean model could be described as having a 'corporatist' approach. The system has been designed by the state, with quite rigid conditions in many cases, but is run in the private sector. This approach is at the root of a number of recently reformed pension systems throughout the world. The UK system is very much influenced by the state but still has many features that have evolved in a pluralist, liberal private sector, such as a diverse range of institutional and benefit structures. At the same time, though, the UK has a complex regulatory and tax system together with a highly complex interaction of means-tested benefits and pension income.

Thus there is a tremendous variety of pension arrangements around the world, depending, *inter alia*, on the size of the private and government sectors, the attitude to regulation, the level of means-tested safety nets, the level of trade union involvement, the ability of private capital markets to survive the two world wars and the tax system. In some countries there are simple, predominantly private systems that operate in a strict framework of rules defining membership, policy terms, etc. (for example, Chile and Australia); in other countries there are relatively straightforward, over-arching state schemes with little role for the private sector (as is the case, for example, in much of continental Europe). The authors believe that, in the UK, reform is possible, enabling return to a simpler deregulated system in which the state plays some role but in which there is a wide variety of forms of private provision. O'Connell (2003) concludes that, 'The UK has one of the most complex state pension system [*sic*].' It is not clear, however, that there are obvious lessons from abroad. Different pensions systems have different combinations of problems, including: high contributions rates; an unfunded pensions burden; high administrative costs; complexity; discouragement of private initiative; low retirement incomes; and encouragement of early retirement or incapacity. There is no one system that can obviously be transplanted from another country to the UK.

6 ISSUES FOR FURTHER ANALYSIS

In Part 1 we have described a system of retirement income provision that appears complex, with many of these complexities being imposed by government. The unnecessary complexity of the pensions system arises partly from attempts to micro-manage the incomes of individuals in different circumstances. The complexity can be illustrated by reference to a simple case. A widow, who had a considerable period out of the labour market to bring up children and who had just two jobs during her working life, could easily be in receipt of: a basic state pension, state second pension, pension credit, council tax benefit, housing benefit, two occupational pensions, a personal pension, a free television licence and winter fuel allowance. That would be ten sources of income, probably adding up to less than £10,000 per annum, for somebody in relatively straightforward circumstances. Seven of those sources of income would come from the government. The number of income sources could easily be greater, and we have ignored income from general savings (such as ISAs) and needs-based benefits such as those provided for long-term care. We have also ignored the separate sources of defined contribution pension income that can exist under different tax codes. If her total income were considerably higher, only three of those sources of income would be removed, but the number could easily be expanded if the individual had more than two jobs. It is difficult to see any economic rationale for the state to provide more than two forms of state retirement income (a state pension and means-tested benefits).

In Part 2 we will look in greater detail at the problems arising from the system of retirement income provision in the UK and identify more precisely policy issues that need to be addressed. In Part 3 we will make policy proposals. Specifically, we will address:

- whether the interaction of the tax system and means-testing system creates serious disincentives to save, as well as an overly complex system;
- the underlying logic of the tax system for pensions and whether the principles on which it is based can be improved;
- whether the role of the state in retirement income provision can be simplified and reduced;
- the regulatory system for pensions and how this can be simplified to reduce the costs of bureaucracy to the state and time costs within the private sector, as well as how it can facilitate more rational economic decision-making by individuals and companies;
- whether individuals (perhaps through collective groups, including trade unions) should be enabled to contract out of further parts of the state pension system;
- whether there should be further compulsory pension provision;
- whether we should try to decouple tax, pensions and social security policy from being age dependent to facilitate greater choice of retirement age and retirement income patterns.

Part 2
The Problems of the Quagmire

In this part we analyse some of the problems caused by the pensions quagmire in greater detail. Means testing, contracting-out provisions, tax regulations and the plethora of different income sources all add to the complexity. Some of these chapters (particularly Chapter 7 and Chapter 8) are necessarily complex. We have simplified the explanations as far as possible but do not wish to leave parts of the system, or their economic implications, unexplained. As was noted in the Introduction, however, the reader interested only in the policy issues could move straight to Part 3 without any loss of continuity.

7 DISINCENTIVES TO SAVE AND TO WORK – MEANS TESTING

Means testing is expected to encompass up to two-thirds of the retired population, in the coming decades, as a result of the introduction of Pension Credit. Many people, particularly those on low earnings, might choose not to save since they expect to be entitled to means-tested benefits in retirement. Those who do save could find that they are no better off in retirement, having had to consume less while in work than they could have done, as a result of saving. Means testing is often viewed as punishing thrift. The issue of means testing has been well covered in the literature, although not all authors have come to similar policy conclusions (see, for example, Clark, 2001; Willetts in Deacon, 2002; Field in Deacon, 2002; and Simpson, 2003).

Means testing also introduces work disincentives. If individuals perceive that further saving is unlikely to be sufficient to take their level of income above means-testing levels they have less incentive to stay in work and accrue pension rights as they approach retirement. Alternatively, having saved, people could choose to retire early and draw down their savings, in the knowledge that, when they reach state pension age, they can rely on means-tested benefits. Effectively, the utility of consuming more while of working age is greater than the utility of the extra consumption that might otherwise have been possible in retirement, since the potential additional consumption in retirement is reduced by means testing (Feldstein, 1987). These views were supported by evidence given to the Select Committee on Social Security by the TUC (SSSC, 1999) and by much of the evidence given to the House of Lords Economic Affairs Committee of Inquiry into Pension Provision (see House of Lords, 2003).

The TUC also states that means testing creates 'an especially perverse work disincentive for female partners of unemployed claimants'. This arises since many women's income is insufficient to support their family, even when in full-time work, so, if a woman's partner becomes unemployed, the logical choice is for the woman to give up work so that both the man and the woman can receive means-tested benefits. This problem arises partly because the unit of assessment for means-tested benefits is the couple, whereas the unit of assessment for tax is the individual. Thus, in the above example, if the woman were to continue working, she would start paying tax on her own earnings, at very low wages, yet her earnings would disqualify both herself and her partner from means-tested benefits. These disincentives also exist in relation to saving and work in retirement. If the male of a couple had no savings, the return to incremental savings derived from a small number of hours' work undertaken by the female might well be zero or negative.

Neumark and Powers have investigated the effect of means testing on work and savings decisions in the USA, using data from the Survey of Income Program Participation. In the USA the federal government provides Supplementary Security Income (SSI) to the elderly (among other recipients) on a means-tested basis. The investigation is of special interest since individual states can choose to supplement federal levels of benefit, or to have different means-testing criteria, and so the relative behaviour of individuals in more or less 'generous' states can be investigated. The studies looked at the work and savings patterns of those men most likely to be eligible for means-tested benefits. They demonstrated that:

- means-testing the SSI discourages work among men nearing retirement age, as might be expected, since the means test penalises both income and assets post age 65 (Neumark and Powers, 1999);
- higher levels of means-tested benefits reduce pre-retirement saving among likely programme participants (Neumark and Powers, 1998).

While the study is based on conditions in the USA, it is not unreasonable to assume that similar conclusions would be drawn from a similar UK study. Age Concern, in evidence to the Select Committee on Social Security (SSSC, 1999), expressed the distress felt by those who, having saved throughout their working lifetime, find that they are little or no better off than they would have been otherwise.

Similar results have been demonstrated using statistical models in the USA. The results of simulations carried out in Friedberg (1999) suggest that eliminating the earnings test applied to SSI would produce a substantial boost to labour supply at minimal fiscal cost.

An argument often used to support means testing is that it affords governments a chance to control spending by targeting it at those groups that most require financial support. Thus, apparently, those with low incomes should be better supported by the social security system, from a less punitive tax system largely contributed to by those on higher incomes. After receiving evidence from the Microsimulation Unit at Cambridge University, however, the Select Committee on Social Security (SSSC, 1999) concluded that 'a wholly means tested system would be cheaper, but would have an unacceptably large number of losers, would have severe consequences on work and savings incentives, and [would lead to] high error rates and fraud'. It has also been demonstrated that, if means-tested benefits make up part of state policy on retirement income, the result is likely to be an increased disparity of wealth among those in retirement (Sefton et al., 1998). That is, means-testing social security actually increases inequality between the rich and the poor.

We make no judgements here about the appropriate level of income redistribution. Indeed, our conclusions would be valid if one believed that social security payments should be given only in very rare cases to those destitute throughout life or, at the other end of the spectrum, if one believed in a formal framework of means-tested benefits that provided significant income enhancement for the less well off. Any method of helping the less well off will involve disincentives to save and work. It is clear from our analysis so far, however, and from the further analysis below, that means testing as used in the UK today now affects large numbers of pensioners – approximately 50 per cent – and the disincentive effects are very severe. The system is sub-optimal and overly complex.

Quantification of the disincentives problem

It is of interest, first, to estimate the value of means-tested benefits to individuals who can expect to receive them. The present value of the MIG, for example (that is, the amount that would have to be invested on reasonable assumptions to produce an income stream equal to the MIG), can be compared with the amount that an individual might reasonably be expected to save during his or her working life. It is reasonably straightforward to estimate the value of the MIG to an individual who retired in 2003, before the introduction of Pension Credit: the total expected present value at age 65 is about £97,000 (see Appendix A for assumptions). The present value of the full, single person's, Basic State Pension (BSP) was about £60,000.[1]

Very few people have a full NIC record and receive 100 per cent of the BSP. On the other hand, many people retiring now will have earned some entitlement under the State Earnings Related Pension Scheme (SERPS). On average, people retiring in 2002 received about 80 per cent of the full BSP and about £30 per week from SERPS. If we offset the value of this income from the value of the MIG the present value of the net means-tested benefits is £25,000.

So during their retirement, an 'average' person who has no savings can expect to receive, in present-value terms, at least £25,000 of means-tested benefits excluding housing or council tax benefit. It should be noted that housing benefit, in particular, is financially very significant for many pensioners. The government pays out about the same in housing benefit as it does in MIG/Pension Credit to those over state pension age.

The other way of looking at this is that an individual would have to save in excess of £25,000 by their state pension age in order to be free of the high marginal rate of tax and benefit

---

1 This calculation assumes the individual retires in January 2003 with a full single person's BSP of £75.50 per week.

withdrawal under the old MIG system. This sum can be regarded as the 'passport' to the basic-rate tax system.[2] Given this, it is quite possible that the lifetime consumption of those on a given income who save will be lower than that of those who do not save. The people likely to fall into this trap, those on low earnings, or with intermittent working histories, may have had to make considerable sacrifices to save during their working life.

From October 2003 the calculation became more difficult. Under the Pension Credit the marginal rate of benefit withdrawal will fall for those with incomes greater than the BSP from 100 to 40 per cent. The coverage increases, however, so that it is possible to be in receipt of this means-tested benefit at a higher level of income. After the introduction of Pension Credit, a larger amount of saving (£61,000) will be required to avoid the 40 per cent benefit withdrawal rate of Pension Credit – again, ignoring the effect of means-tested benefits in kind. Two further points should be made about benefits in kind, which it is impossible to incorporate in these calculations because their impact varies from person to person. First, given their level, it would not be unreasonable to assume that, in many cases, an individual would have to save £100,000 to be free of means testing. Second, the saving of £61,000 to purchase an annuity that would allow a person to avoid being in receipt of Pension Credit would only take many such savers into the even higher levels of benefit withdrawal seen when housing and council tax benefit are withdrawn.

The savings required to 'beat' the means test will vary according to each individual's working history. But a stark example of how thrift is discouraged for those on low earnings is

---

2   Ignoring the effect of the withdrawal of the age allowance (see below).

Table 3 **Return on saving for someone on minimum wage saving £20 per month**

	Number of years of work and saving			
	10	20	30	40
Real investment return	Actual return, net of the Pension Credit			
2%	–10%	–3%	–1%	–1%
4%	–7%	–1%	1%	2%
6%	–5%	1%	3%	5%

given by the figures in Table 3. It shows, for different levels of real rate of return on an individual's savings of £20 per month, the real rate of return after adjusting for the loss of Pension Credit caused by the saving, where participation in the labour force and saving take place for various different lengths of time. The adjusted rate of return involves calculating the real rate of return after having subtracted the value of the lost Pension Credit from the individual's accumulated saving. For example, someone on the minimum wage throughout their lives, who worked for 30 years and received a real return of 4 per cent (substantially higher than the risk-free real rate of return net of expenses available in investment markets today), would have that return reduced to 1 per cent after allowing for the loss of means-tested benefits. It should be remembered that this understates the true problem because the loss of housing and council tax benefit are ignored. Some of the other examples from the table are even more stark.

It is worth making three further points relating to this analysis. This situation would seem to encourage what would normally be irrational risk-taking as, once real returns are sufficient to take an individual out of the Pension Credit, the individual will gain from further upside increases in return but not lose so much from lower returns, because of the cushion of means-tested benefit: thus moral hazard encourages risk-taking by those least able to bear the cost. Also, it appears that much of the apparent tax advantage of pension saving is nullified by the impact of means testing. Third, the individual has an incentive to spend all their tax-free cash lump sum, rather than use it to buy a pension. By spending it they will be able to receive means-tested benefits and the benefits of the lump sum. If it is assumed that the tax-free lump sum were spent in this way, it would raise the rates of returns net of pension credit that we quoted in Part 1. The saving would only be transitory, however, and would not be used to provide a retirement income. By a similar argument this situation makes saving through ISAs relatively more attractive than pensions because, when the individual's circumstances are known at retirement, a decision can be taken to spend down savings from ISAs if that increases entitlement to means-tested benefits.

There are clearly inadequacies in using the approach of considering individuals in particular situations to illustrate the problem of means testing. Notwithstanding the inadequacies of examining stylised examples, it is, however, effective in conveying the structure of incentives faced by individual decision-makers. In Part 1, we noted that, while the government concentrated on aggregate figures (40 per cent of pension income to be received from the state, for example), the picture when we considered individual quintiles of the income distribution looked very different, for all quintiles, from that of the average. Very often more can be hidden in aggregate figures than is revealed, and therefore the approach of examining individual cases can be helpful.

A further way of illustrating the problems of the interaction of means-tested benefits with pensions income is to look at marginal rates of tax and benefit withdrawal across the income spectrum.

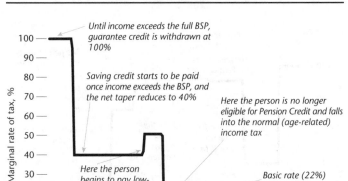

Figure 3   **Marginal tax rates for a single person with BSP £60 per week — no housing benefit or council tax benefit**

This approach illustrates both the problem of means testing and disincentives, and the problem of complexity. In Figures 3 and 4, we show the rate of withdrawal of private income, due to means testing and income tax as income increases from a basic state pension of £60 (less than that received for a full working life). Figure 3 shows the marginal rates of tax and benefit withdrawal assuming the only means-tested benefit received is the Pension Credit. Figure 4 shows the marginal tax rates and benefit withdrawal rates assuming the person is also entitled to receive housing and council tax benefit.

There are seven different rates of tax and benefit withdrawal, some of them extremely high and applying to moderate incomes.

Figure 4   **Marginal tax rates for a single person with BSP of £60 per week – paying rent of £200 per month and £600 in council tax**

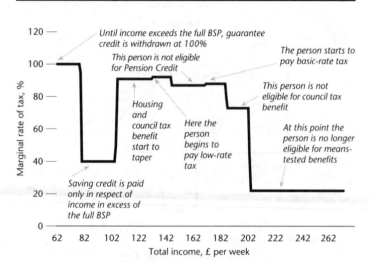

Individuals in receipt of the Pension Credit only will not reach the normal tax system permanently until their income is over £145 per week, but even then they are still in receipt of other means-tested benefits. If such a person had a full basic state pension plus £30 per week SERPS/S2P, private savings of about £75,000 would be needed to buy an annuity to start retirement in the normal tax system. We are considering only those on moderate incomes in this section, but this situation of high marginal rates of tax and benefit withdrawal continues as income rises and special age-dependent tax allowances are withdrawn: there is a brief discussion of this particular issue in Part 3.

We also need to consider the evolution of the system over the

Figure 5   **Difference between amount of state pensions and Pension Credit, by year of retirement**
Start salary £18,000, S2P capped, £

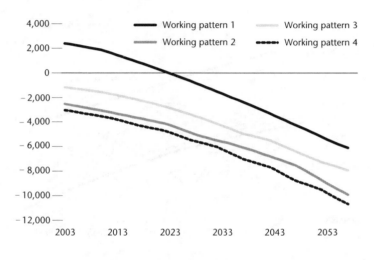

long term. The current arrangements have a built-in bias towards more means testing. The Pension Credit is expected to increase in line with earnings, while the BSP increases only in line with prices. Thus each subsequent generation will have to save more in order to have a retirement income greater than means-tested levels. Figures 5 and 6 show the difference between the income provided by state benefits (the BSP, SERPS and the state second pension (S2P)) and the Upper Income Threshold for Pension Credit eligibility for people retiring between 2003 and 2050, assuming that policy evolves as the government has indicated it believes it should.

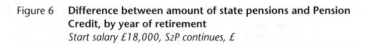

Figure 6   **Difference between amount of state pensions and Pension Credit, by year of retirement**
Start salary £18,000, S2P continues, £

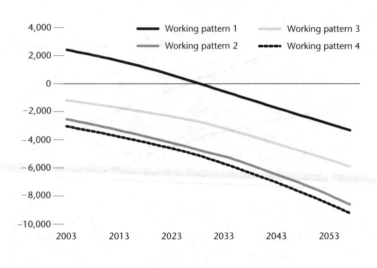

'S2P capped' (Figure 5) covers the case where accrual under the proposed state second pension stops being earnings related from 2010, as the government intended in 1998; 'S2P continues' (Figure 6) assumes that accrual continues to be earnings related. Figure 6 would also demonstrate the effect for those who contract out if rebates given to those who contract out of S2P remain earnings related yet S2P were capped.

The working patterns are:

- working pattern 1 – full-time paid employment between ages 18 and 65;

- working pattern 2 – full-time paid employment between ages 18 and 28 followed by a short break and some part-time and full-time paid employment until age 55;
- working pattern 3 – full-time paid employment between ages 23 and 65 apart from a break between ages 32 and 37;
- working pattern 4 – intermittent full-time paid employment throughout a working lifetime.

A more detailed explanation of the terms and the derivation of the assumptions used to produce the figures is provided in Cooper (1997).[3]

Figures 5 and 6 show how larger groups of people will be permanently trapped in the means-testing system if they rely on BSP plus the proceeds of S2P or a stakeholder pension financed by contracted-out rebates. They will also need larger amounts of savings to extract themselves from the means-testing system as means-tested benefits increase in real terms and relative to other benefits. The government's aim of gradually reducing the coverage of means-tested benefits is very unlikely to be achieved under these circumstances. An implicit assumption of these charts is that rebates from S2P are actuarially neutral so that an individual does not gain in expected-value terms by contracting out, although in fact the rebates are now viewed as being worse than neutral (see, for example, Cooper, 2004).

We now repeat the calculations above, demonstrating the cost of the 'passport' to the non-means-tested part of the system for longer time horizons and using different work

---

3 The figures have been updated, of course, since Cooper (1997).

histories. The income provided by BSP and S2P for someone retiring in the year 2003, having completed 'working pattern 2', is £660 per annum less than the guarantee credit. This person would need savings of £29,000 to provide an income equivalent to the guarantee credit, or £65,000 to provide an income in excess of the upper threshold for Pension Credit, throughout their retirement. If the individual is entitled to other means-tested benefits, such as housing or council tax credit, the savings needed to be above the means-testing net will be higher. By 2025 the gap in income has increased to nearly £2,000 per annum, which would require savings of £103,000 to 'beat' the Pension Credit threshold. By 2050 savings of £166,000 would be required. All these figures are in *current* purchasing power terms. These calculations are illustrated in Figure 7, including the cost of housing and council tax benefit. They ignore the likelihood of increasing annuity costs due to increased longevity.

Figure 7 illustrates how future generations of pensioners face a widening gap between state pension provision and means-tested benefits owing to the different rates at which the guarantee credit, the Pension Credit upper limit and the BSP are proposed to be increased. Thus the disincentive effects prevail over a wide range of income and assets. Means-tested benefits also affect other decisions to do with retirement income. The rational decision, for example, might be to use pensions savings to purchase a fixed pension at 65, use all other available assets for current consumption and then rely on the Pension Credit in older age. There is a strong incentive to spend any lump sums immediately.

Means testing also makes the savings decisions of people

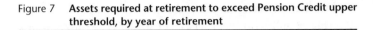

Figure 7   Assets required at retirement to exceed Pension Credit upper threshold, by year of retirement

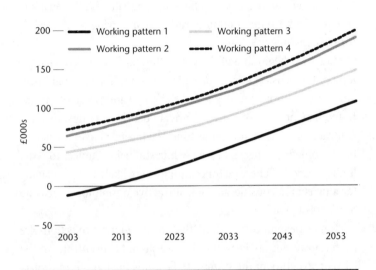

on low incomes and those with intermittent working histories considerably more difficult. The 'best advice' for these individuals might be not to make pension savings beyond compulsory levels, since the likelihood is that their value will be undermined by means-tested benefits. Other forms of saving might be preferable, as individuals can then choose how to spend the money if they reach retirement and use the money to maximise entitlement to means-tested benefits, given the rules that prevail at the time of their retirement. Thus the whole means-testing apparatus may undermine completely the structure of retirement income provision for those individuals (the majority) who are likely to be in receipt of means-tested benefits in retirement. It is highly unlikely that the tax treatment of pensions, relative to other forms of saving, is sufficiently beneficial (see Chapter 11) to offset the loss to individuals of means-tested benefits that will arise if they are in receipt of a retirement annuity rather than having more flexible forms of saving.

Since the beginning of the 1980s, the state has scaled back the level of the pension benefit provided in return for national insurance contributions but expanded the scope and range of means-tested benefits and encouraged private pension savings, through contracting out. At the same time, saving in pension schemes has become more heavily taxed, while still being subject to strict limits on access. These factors combined are likely to make saving for a pension a considerably less attractive option for increasing numbers of people.

It may be tempting to think that the long-term projections are irrelevant to our analysis and that we should concentrate on the current structure of the system. In fact, it is the long-term projections which are more important. It is true that means-testing systems do affect the behaviour of individuals today – for example, they affect whether to save, whether to move to a smaller house, whether to continue working, etc. In so far as long-term pension saving is concerned, however, it is savers' rational expectations of the development of the system which are important. It is often thought that savers need to be protected by large amounts of regulation relating to product-selling to prevent them from behaving irrationally. The analysis suggests, however, that people on low incomes are behaving perfectly rationally by not saving! Indeed, one remarkable feature of the recent Turner Report, published by the Pensions Commission (see Introduction), is that it suggested that a difficulty of a market in pensions is that people generally do not behave rationally with regard to pension provision. Yet there is a huge amount of evidence, including that cited in the Turner Report, to suggest that individuals, facing the labyrinthine quagmire of the state pensions and benefits system, are behaving perfectly rationally by reducing their pension provision and not saving sufficient amounts to be independent of means-tested benefits in retirement.

Incentives for early retirement

As is clear from the work of Hannah (1986), the concept of a retirement age was not invented by the state. It developed through the hierarchical and frequently paternalistic labour markets of companies in the nineteenth century. The concept of a 'retirement age' has been reinforced by the state over the course of the twentieth century. The most explicit mechanism by which this has been so is through the state pension age, although, arguably, other elements of government policy are more important in encouraging retirement at a specific age (or earlier).

Before looking at the ways in which governments have institutionalised retirement, it is worth considering a hypothetical market in which all employees are members of defined contribution pension schemes and there is no state pension scheme. Social security payments are assumed to be at subsistence levels at all ages, although needs-based payments might also be made (for example, to meet long-term care or disability needs). It is quite clear that, in this environment, at an individual level and ignoring corporate reorganisations within the workforce, workers could retire when they chose to. They could balance the gain, in terms of extra income (and ultimately higher pension income), from continuing to work with the value of extra leisure time. Retirement may take place gradually, with the pension 'pot' being used to even out income during the period of gradual retirement. This would seem to allow individuals to optimise their own retirement decisions.[4]

Such a situation also facilitates the adjustment of the economy as a whole to changing preferences, demographic structures, and so on. As a population ages and individuals start drawing down on their pension savings, the capital-to-labour ratio will change. A detailed modelling and analysis of such a change in the UK has been undertaken by Miles (1999). Miles's conclusions confirm economic intuition. As the capital-to-labour ratio rises, relative wages rise and returns to capital fall. Individuals can respond to these relative price changes. The most likely response to these changes in the labour market is an increase in labour supply (either through later retirement or more gradual retirement). Thus the rational economic reactions to the price signals precipitated by changes in population structure lead individuals to respond in ways that may make them more likely to increase labour supply. It follows that impediments on individuals reacting in this way will lead to sub-optimal behaviour.

The most explicit impediment to price signals encouraging later or gradual retirement as the population structure changes appears to be the basic state pension. Prior to the basic state pension age most people are in paid employment; after it, the vast majority are not. State pensions can be deferred, however, and are enhanced for late payment. While this option is not widely

---

4   This is not an argument for or against defined benefit or defined contribution pension schemes. The exposition of the argument is simpler if we assume a defined contribution world.

advertised, state pension age need not act as an impediment to the informed employee making rational choices about retirement age.[5]

A more serious artificial encouragement to earlier-than-optimal retirement arises from the regulations surrounding the operation of pension schemes. Occupational pension scheme members cannot simultaneously draw their pension while continuing in the same employment, which discourages partial retirement. The Finance Act 2004 will remove this restriction from April 2006.

The Pension Credit provides further encouragement to retire early. Means-tested benefits are now much higher after the age of 65 than before, so, for those on moderate means, there is an incentive to retire at that age. Members of defined contribution schemes have an incentive to retire earlier and receive a lower pension if that qualifies them for means-tested benefits later in life; and there will be less incentive for individuals who will be subject to means testing to work for longer and accumulate greater pension rights.

Thus the current framework for retirement income provision in the UK would seem to encourage retirement at the age of 65 and also encourage retirement before age 65. As such it impedes market forces from responding to labour market shortages as the population ages. In Part 3 we discuss ways in which these incentives to earlier retirement can be reduced.

---

5   Since the late payment enhancement is no more than neutral in respect of the benefit forgone there is little incentive for most people to defer payment of state pensions. The government (Pensions Act 2004) has increased the rate of enhancement, however, so that there will be a genuine incentive to defer payment.

8 S2P, SERPS AND NATIONAL INSURANCE REBATES: MEDDLING, MUDDLING AND WORK DISINCENTIVES

Eligibility for state pension depends on an individual's history of national insurance contributions (NICs), rather than it being means tested, and so even the wealthiest pensioner is in receipt of this income. NICs are effectively a tax on labour. To the extent that they result in labour being taxed more heavily than capital, they could be viewed as introducing bias into employers' decisions as to whether to invest in capital or labour. Any reduction in NICs therefore reduces the effect of this bias. On the other hand, it could be argued that, because NICs give rise to a state pension entitlement (either BSP and/or S2P), they do not represent an effective tax on labour and that they are an insurance premium not a tax. That argument is now difficult to substantiate. The existence of home responsibilities' protection in the BSP and the crediting of full S2P to certain non-earners and low earners means that NICs now have more or less the same marginal impact as a tax because contributions are now not closely related to benefits.

SERPS provided a pension related to an individual's revalued career-average earnings and its underlying principles were straightforward. Whereas the flat-rate basic state pension has an income redistribution role, SERPS conferred an additional state pension based on earnings. As evidenced by contracting out, it provided a quasi-occupational pension arrangement for those employees whose employer was not able or not prepared to provide one directly. Both the instruments and objectives of policy were reasonably clear:

- economic and political debates on the role and mechanism of redistribution would tend to focus on the basic state pension and means-tested benefits;
- debates on the role of the market and the state in pension provision for those who expected incomes above means-testing limits would be focused on SERPS.

For example, debates about the ability of the market to provide earnings-related pensions were most pertinent to the role of SERPS. The scaling down of SERPS and the widening of the opting-out provisions were decisions taken as a result of views that were held by the then government on those particular issues.

The replacement of SERPS by S2P blurs this distinction, since it is designed to perform the role of income redistribution as well as remaining earnings related. The rates of accrual are set so that anybody with earnings above the Upper Earnings Threshold (UET, defined in Part 1) will receive the same rate of pension accrual as promised by SERPS. Anybody earning between the Lower Earnings Threshold (LET) and Upper Earnings Threshold will receive a higher rate of accrual, and anybody below the Lower Earnings Threshold will receive a pension accrual based on the assumption that they were earning the Lower Earnings Threshold.

The first problem is that the system is complicated and unlikely to be understood by most people. Furthermore, it confuses the previously clear and distinct roles of the BSP and SERPS. For those earning below the LET, S2P effectively represents an extra flat-rate state pension (although with different accrual and up-rating conditions from the BSP). For those earning above the LET, it provides an extra flat-rate state pension plus a small earnings-related supplement.

Third, the rebates for contracting out of S2P are not now directly based on the S2P benefit forgone, unlike the SERPs rebates. For example, those earning below the LET will receive a rebate for contracting out that is proportional to their actual earnings, although their S2P entitlement is flat rate. To compensate, those who contract out accrue an S2P 'top-up' to the benefit provided by their rebate. Those who are contracted out via an occupational scheme will continue to pay reduced-rate NICs as though they were contracted out of SERPS, and so everyone in such schemes earning less than the UET will also receive an S2P 'top-up'. This whole process involves considerable administrative and transactions costs, as well as costs to individuals for whom financial decisions are made even more complicated. It is difficult to imagine most individuals actually being able to perform calculations to determine whether they have been given the correct level of S2P at retirement.

It is proposed that at some stage S2P should become flat rate. This means that all those remaining in the system will accrue pension based on the assumption that they earned the LET. It is also proposed, however, that rebates will remain earnings related. The problems mentioned above, for those earning below the LET, remain. Those earning much above the LET will have a clear incentive to contract out. S2P then appears to become an instrument of redistribution, although since the contracting-out rebate is earnings related the extent of this is confused.

For those who do not contract out, flat-rate S2P will be very little different from the BSP. A second basic state pension will have been created with a completely separate set of rules and administrative systems.

The decoupling of rebates from the rates of pension accrual, and the further erosion of the relationship between NICs and benefits received, will cause an effective increase in labour market taxes.[1] Under SERPS, an additional pound of earnings between the lower and upper earnings limits led to additional national insurance liability and additional SERPS accrual. Under S2P, if an individual acquires an additional pound of earnings, additional S2P accrual will not necessarily take place but additional NICs will still be incurred. The additional SERPS accrual when an individual acquires an extra pound of earnings was estimated by the Government Actuary to be worth about 5 pence (on average – the combined employer and employee NI rebate for schemes contracted out on a defined benefit basis is 5.1 per cent). By opting out of SERPS this 5 pence could, in effect, be rebated in cash, as long as it was then invested in an appropriate personal pension scheme. Under S2P, below the LET, there will be no additional S2P accrual from an additional pound of earnings. If somebody has opted out of S2P, they will receive an additional national insurance rebate, but this will be cancelled out by the loss of earnings-related S2P.

So, because individuals no longer receive a proportional benefit for their additional NICs, effective labour market taxes are increased by about 2.5 per cent between the LET and the UET and

---

1   The explanation that follows may seem to the reader like the sort of complex explanation that gets actuaries a bad name. However, the fact that British pensions
are a 21st-century version of the Schleswig-Holstein dispute is entirely the fault of
HM Government.

by about 5 per cent below the LET, depending on the person's age. This argument may seem arcane; it is certainly highly complex. That is only because the sheer complexity of the system obscures the underlying economic effect on individuals, however. It is possible that the decision to increase labour market taxes in this way was a conscious and deliberate decision taken by the government and that it balanced the impact on incentives with the benefits, in the government's eyes, of further redistribution. If this was the case, there was no explicit reference to this issue whatsoever in the 1998 Green Paper.

Thus the shift from SERPS to S2P has involved moving from a straightforward system where people paid an earnings-related NIC to receive accrual of an earnings-related pension to one where there is no clear relationship between the pension accrued, the level of earnings and the level of contribution. We have also moved from a situation where individuals could give up their rights to pension accrual in return for a rebate of NICs proportionate to the benefit forgone to one where the rebate does not necessarily relate to the pension forgone. This complexity will increase if and when S2P becomes flat rate. We consider how to address this problem in Part 3.

Problems caused by rules for contracting out of SERPS/S2P

The regulatory costs of contracting out have grown out of all proportion to the benefit provided by the regulations. Originally the intention was that schemes that contracted out of SERPS should be required to provide a minimum level of benefit (the Guaranteed Minimum Pension – GMP). Periodic checks were made of the funding levels of contracted-out schemes in order to ensure that the liability for the GMP was covered.

Subsequently, concerns about preservation, transfer values and indexation of benefits have increased the complexity of administering contracted-out schemes. In addition, the SERPS formula and the calculation of GMP were changed in 1988 and new contracted-out regimes were introduced in 1997, so that there are several tranches of benefit that have to be considered.

S2P introduces further complexity. Even before S2P becomes flat rate, however, a large proportion of the day-to-day administration costs of pension schemes is being driven by a minor part of the benefit.

Pickering (2002), as part of a major report into the simplification of occupational pension schemes, suggested considerable simplification of contracting-out rules. Others have argued that contracting out should not be allowed at all and that a larger flat-rate state pension benefit be made available. We discuss this further in Part 3.

A profusion of other rules also causes complexity for occupational pension schemes. The requirements of the 1995 Pensions Act, the regulations that arise from the European Court of Justice and European Court of Human Rights, regulations relating to ethical investment and so on can be onerous and always impose relatively greater costs on smaller employers. It is not necessarily easy for the UK government to deal with regulations arising from other jurisdictions, but there could be a considerable simplification of other types of legislation.

9 PROBLEMS WITH STAKEHOLDER PENSIONS

Stakeholder pensions were launched in April 2001. They are CAT-marked products – that is, subject to regulations relating to 'cost', 'access' and 'terms'.

The main aspects of CAT marking are:

- Charges must be expressed as a percentage of the fund and are limited to 1 per cent of the fund per annum. An additional charge can be made if investment advice is provided.[1]
- The Financial Services Authority (FSA) regulates stakeholder pension plans in conjunction with OPRA (the Occupational Pensions Regulatory Authority), but because stakeholder plans are CAT-marked there is perceived to be less need for individually tailored advice on their sale. The FSA has published 'decision trees' to help individuals make choices with regard to stakeholder pensions and standard information should be provided across all stakeholder products.
- Stakeholder plans must accept business from anybody wishing to contribute at least £20 per month.
- Employers with five or more 'relevant' employees must select

---

1   There are likely to be changes to the regulation to allow an additional 0.5 per cent charge in the first ten years to finance the initial set-up costs.

and provide access to a designated stakeholder pension for all their 'relevant employees'.

Up-front fees cannot be charged when a policy commences and no exit penalty can be charged. Stakeholder purchasers with small funds pay lower fees in total than those with larger funds.

These regulations, in effect, amount to price control. There is no compulsion on insurers to provide the product, however. One would expect to see under-supply of products subject to such controls, assuming that prices were set below the level that would prevail in a competitive market (as, for example, happened during the period of rent control in the private-rented housing market). This does not seem to have happened in the market for stakeholder pensions. In August 2003 there were 48 stakeholder providers listed as registered on OPRA's website, although only thirteen had completely unrestricted access (see also Part 1). In 2001 and 2002 there had been 53 registered providers[2] and two of those, which subsequently withdrew, were 'empty boxes': that is, they had no members. There are a number of possible explanations as to why there were more providers than might be expected of such price-controlled products:

- The maximum price is above the price that would prevail in a competitive market but the market was not competitive when charges were higher in pre-stakeholder days.
- The average maximum price for all purchasers of the product is sufficient to cover costs, even though, for some purchasers,

---

2   OPRA annual reports.

the price may not cover costs. This situation will lead to other problems, discussed below.

- Providers are willing to cross-subsidise the product to help promote the sale of other products.

- Providers are able to sell products that do not provide an economic return on capital because they believe that other providers will drop out when the product is proven to be uneconomic, leading a few providers to dominate the market, at lower unit cost.

Assuming that the total price paid by a group of 'average' consumers was sufficient for a pension provider to cover average costs, there will be two major forms of cross-subsidy within the group which could lead to serious problems in the development of the stakeholder pensions market. The first of these problems was identified by Mark Boleat when Director General of the ABI; he did not seem to feel the insurance industry could justify charging expenses at a fixed percentage of the fund (see Boleat, 1998) as required in a stakeholder pension. He believed this would involve cross-subsidies from higher to lower contributors and that pension providers would target their marketing efforts at high-earning consumers as such consumers pay relatively more for the product.

So long as providers remain willing to sell stakeholder pensions, this dichotomy, whereby pension providers may wish to direct marketing towards those for whom the product is least good value, may explain the relatively low take-up (1.25 million policies had been sold in total by August 2003, but annual sales have fallen since 2001 – ABI, 2003).

In the long term, high earners may use alternatives to

stakeholder pensions, while stakeholder pensions would be relatively good value for those on low incomes who may use the products for small levels of saving. This would raise average administrative costs, preventing the intended cross-subsidy from high-level contributors to low-level contributors from being effective and leading to withdrawal by providers from the market.

Because pension providers cannot charge directly for set-up costs or the costs of exit, there will be cross-subsidies between those who switch policies between providers and those who remain with one provider. The former group will not contribute fully to the costs of their switching activity. Indeed, it is not clear that a policy-holder who remains with one pension provider throughout the life of a plan will be more favourably treated under the stakeholder price limits than under products sold under the previous regime. A provider meeting the stakeholder criteria could deduct a management charge of 1 per cent per annum of the value of the fund. An alternative provider, under the personal pension regime, might charge a fixed fee of £2 per month and a management charge of 0.5 per cent of the fund per annum. After a 'full working lifetime' of 49 years, someone contributing £240 per annum (an extremely small sum) would be worse off under the stakeholder arrangement by £200 (in present-value terms). By removing the ability to charge a policy set-up fee or exit fee, the benefits of customer loyalty cannot be passed on to the policy-holder in the stakeholder regime. There is therefore no incentive for customer loyalty and total costs could rise as a result of increased switching activity.

The above problems arise from cross-subsidies within the group of stakeholder pension purchasers. If the product as a whole is unprofitable, it might only be sold by companies willing to cross-subsidise the product using the profits from other products. Such cross-subsidies could arise in a market that was not fully competitive. For example, it is difficult for with-profit policy-holders, who are the notional owners of a mutual insurance company, to exercise effective control over the management. The management, whose objectives may relate to sales maximisation rather than maximising the return on with-profit policy-holders' funds, may cross-subsidise the sale of stakeholder pensions, using accumulated capital, or return on capital, which belongs to with-profit policy-holders. One group of customers then benefits at the expense of another. Stakeholder pensions could be used as loss leaders by companies that wish to use them as a marketing device, to obtain other forms of business. Dominant players in the market, with a wide product range, are more likely to use stakeholder pensions in this way.

All these elements of cross-subsidy can damage economic welfare. In particular, they can prevent entry into the market by new providers. Indeed, it is interesting that a practice of cross-subsidising one product or group of consumers with another, which has often been declared illegal by the Competition Commission or the Office of Fair Trading in other markets, is being made compulsory in the pensions market.

10 THE TAX TREATMENT OF PENSION FUNDS AND TAX REGULATIONS

The tax environment within which pension funds operate is an important aspect of the political economy of pension provision. We can consider the tax position from at least three angles. First, there is the framework for taxing savings in general. Then there is the particular tax treatment of pension saving. Finally, we can look at the way in which the tax system operates, in terms of its simplicity, bureaucratic burden on taxpayers, etc.

Alternative tax treatments of savings

Economists often distinguish between two types of tax system: a comprehensive income tax system and an expenditure tax system (see Meade, 1978). A comprehensive income tax taxes all sources of income explicitly. In its most comprehensive form it will also tax sources of imputed income, such as imputed rental income from owner-occupied houses and also accrued but unrealised capital gains. An expenditure tax, on the other hand, taxes only consumption. Effectively an expenditure tax exempts returns from savings from tax until they are consumed.

There are two main forms of expenditure tax. The first involves giving tax relief on income that is saved, exempting from tax any interest and capital gains accumulating on those savings, but then taxing the proceeds of saving as and when they are withdrawn for consumption. This form is often described as EET, with E denoting an exemption or relief from tax and T denoting a point at which tax is payable (the first letter denotes the contribution or investment stage, the second the accumulation stage and the third the drawdown stage). It is often – indeed, perhaps normally – suggested that pension provision in the UK is taxed in this way (see, for example, De Ryck, 1996). As will be discussed below, however, this is an inaccurate description of the system.

Individual savings accounts (ISAs) generally follow the other main form of expenditure tax regime: no relief is given for the investment, but the accumulating interest and gains and the proceeds of the investment are exempt from tax. This system is often described as TEE.

In a tax system that is neither progressive nor regressive, EET produces an equivalent outcome to TEE, although the timing and pattern of tax payments differ between the two. Examples illustrating the equivalence between these forms and other forms of expenditure tax (such as giving investment relief for company investments) are given in Meade (1978). In progressive tax systems, however, different forms of expenditure tax are not equivalent (see, for example, Knox, 1990; Booth and Cooper, 2002).

The arguments as to whether income or expenditure should be used as a tax base have been rehearsed *inter alia* by economists such as Hobbes, Mill, Fisher and Kaldor. A more recent discussion of the economic arguments in favour of using an expenditure tax base is found in Kay and King (1990). They suggest that an expenditure tax treats two individuals the same, regardless of when they choose to consume the income they earn, whereas a comprehensive income tax gives rise to the double taxation of savings. This is because a comprehensive income tax taxes income when it is earned and also taxes interest on savings before the money is spent. In the case of pensions, therefore, it can be argued that an income tax system taxes post-retirement consumption more than pre-retirement consumption. The main economic point in the debate, however, concerns the distortion of decisions to consume or save. An expenditure tax allows individuals to receive interest gross of tax. They can therefore determine their preferences for consumption now or in the future without distortions imposed by the tax system. By contrast, a comprehensive income tax (TTE) (where returns to saving are taxed) would create such distortions, with associated inefficiencies.

There is an alternative argument, however. When wages are saved they become another factor of production (capital). It can be argued that the returns to all factors of production should be taxed equally. Taxes just on expenditure are equivalent to taxes just on wages with no tax on returns to capital.[1] A tax just on wages distorts the work/leisure decision in the same way that a tax on capital distorts the save/consume decision. To tax returns to labour but not tax returns to capital encourages those engaged in production to use less labour and more capital. It would seem reasonable, looking only at these economic arguments, to tax the

---

1   This argument is not always clearly understood. It is often suggested that EET does tax returns from capital because tax is ultimately paid on all the benefits received from saving. The equivalence of EET with TEE, however, demonstrates that tax is not being paid on returns to capital under EET. It is clear that returns to capital are not taxed by TEE because no tax is paid on interest at any stage. If TEE and EET are equivalent, tax cannot be paid on returns to capital in the EET case either. In EET, it is true that tax is paid on the total accumulated fund, when it is paid out as a benefit. The tax is also deferred on the whole of the fund, however: the two effects cancel out, leaving the equivalent, in present-value terms, of a tax just on returns to labour.

returns to all factors of production. This would suggest a comprehensive income tax base rather than an expenditure tax base. This is the most powerful argument against an EET basis for the taxation of pension funds. Tax revenues have to be raised; the question is whether the consumption/savings decision should be distorted to the same extent or to a lesser extent than the work/leisure decision.

Taxation of pension funds

In one sense, pension funds have the same economic characteristics as general savings: they represent a fund of financial assets and capital giving rise to investment returns. In an institutional and legal sense, however, pension funds are distinct from general savings. They are collective funds of non-returnable contributions; they are mutual insurance funds (in the case of defined benefit schemes and annuitised defined contribution schemes); and they represent deferred pay. While the general discussion about the taxation of savings is relevant to pensions, there are additional considerations which should be taken into account. One of these is the impact of inflation.

Whether tax systems should include indexation or other adjustments for inflation has been discussed *inter alia* in Meade (1978), Kay and King (1990) and Fabian Society (1990). Most countries tax the nominal return on investments (Denmark is an exception). As is shown in Booth and Cooper (2000), for example, a tax on nominal returns can reduce a real return from 3 to 1 per cent at only a 6 per cent rate of inflation. Taxation of nominal returns represents, in effect, taxation of capital or double taxation of previously earned income. Capital gains tax, in respect of company shares, can also be a double tax. In so far as a rise in a share's value takes place owing to retained profits, the investor is taxed twice: once on the tax levied on the profits and once on the capital gain that arises from the retention.

A tax on real returns would probably be difficult to operate in practice, so governments might have to choose between taxing the nominal return and exempting investment returns from tax completely. In the case of pension funds, where money has to be 'locked up' for considerable periods of time, it might be better to err on the side of not taxing at all. The alternative of taxing interest income at income tax rates (or at a pension fund provider's corporation tax rate) would, in times of high inflation, lead to an unintentional and unplanned erosion of capital, with serious financial consequences. This issue may seem esoteric but it was, in fact, the main reason why tax-free accumulation of pension fund assets was granted in 1921, after the experience of the inflation of the period during and shortly after World War I. Even low rates of inflation can give rise to significant erosion of real capital in a comprehensive income tax system based on taxing nominal returns to saving.

Fiscal encouragement for pension provision can also be justified on the grounds that means-tested benefits in old age discourage some people (until recently only people on low incomes but now the majority of the population) from making their own pension provision. Le Grand and Agulnik (1998) write, 'Thus direct spending on universal pensions ... acts as a positive disincentive for personal savings; a disincentive effect that is further complicated if the pension is not universal but income and asset-tested.' This provides a further argument in favour of EET.

EET, TEE or TTE for pension funds?

One feature of the EET form of expenditure tax, in a progressive tax system, as compared with the TEE form, is that EET allows individuals to minimise the tax they pay by spreading their income. Thus, people can make contributions to pension schemes when they are paying higher-rate tax (obtaining relief at 40 per cent) and then receive the pension when they are paying tax at the basic rate. Fabian Society (1990) seems to suggest that such income spreading is not a desirable feature of the tax system (although recognising the impracticality of eliminating it). This is a curious view to take when the very purpose of pension schemes is to spread income (after tax) more evenly over a person's lifetime.

The authors would argue that it is desirable for individuals to have the ability to spread income across their lifetime and this should be recognised for tax purposes. In any event, the purpose of a progressive tax system, if one believes in that principle, is that those with the ability to do so should pay more tax. In principle, it is lifetime income and not annual income which is the better measure of the lifetime ability to pay tax and which should be taxed in a progressive way. Deferring pay through a pension fund is one way of levelling out annual income so that each year's income (after deducting pension contributions and adding in pension payments) is a fairer representation of lifetime income. Individual contributors to pension funds, particularly the self-employed, can also use pension contributions to 'spread' their net income for tax purposes.

Saving through pension funds involves individuals forgoing consumption for a substantial period of time (several decades and the lifetime of ten to fifteen governments). If we accept that it is an aim of government to promote independent pension provision, to prevent people from relying on the state in old age, then pension funds may need to have greater certainty of tax regime and a more favourable tax regime than other types of saving. Thus, even if all forms of saving do not follow an expenditure tax regime, the authors believe that pensions should do so. Furthermore, we believe that the particular expenditure tax regime that is appropriate is EET.

The tax treatment of pensions in practice

To what extent is the current tax treatment of pensions the EET system, as is so commonly supposed?[2] The tax position of contributions and benefits in both defined contribution and defined benefit schemes is described below.

Contributions

In the case of occupational schemes, whether defined benefit or defined contribution, full tax relief is given on all employer's contributions but there are limits on benefits (see below). Employees receive tax relief on contributions up to 15 per cent of capped earnings (£102,000 in 2004/5) for that tax year. Employees can also make additional voluntary contributions (AVCs) as long as the total contribution does not exceed 15 per cent of earnings and as long as benefits do not breach the benefit ceilings (see

---

2   Although the Inland Revenue proposed major structural changes to the tax regime for pensions in its consultation document (Inland Revenue, 2002), and formalised these in the Finance Act 2004, this does not change the argument in this section, since for most people what is taxed and when it is taxed will not be affected.

below). Contributions to a personal pension scheme can be made with full tax relief, up to an age-related maximum contribution rate, starting at 17.5 per cent of capped earnings. Personal pension schemes can allow a contribution of up to £3,600 (including basic-rate tax relief), regardless of earnings.

Concurrent membership of an occupational and personal pension scheme is permitted only for those paid less than £30,000 (in 2004/5).[3]

Investment returns

Investment income is exempt from tax in the sense that no further tax is paid once the income is in the hands of the fund. In the case of investments in bonds, property and cash, any tax deducted at source is reclaimable by the pension fund, so the entire return is tax free. In the case of investments in equities, however, profits are taxed at source in the company's hands and this tax cannot be reclaimed by the pension fund. Prior to the July 1997 Budget, a tax credit was available for that part of the return from UK equities received in the form of dividends, but this is no longer given. The tax rate suffered by pension funds on equities is thus the UK corporation tax rate (in general, 30 per cent from 2004/5) or, in the case of overseas equities, the equivalent tax rate of the foreign country plus any non-reclaimable withholding tax.

---

3   These limits will be removed from tax year 2006/7, under the Finance Act 2004; a very high ceiling on tax-free contributions will apply which will affect relatively few people.

Benefits

Benefits taken in pension form are taxed at normal income tax rates. The maximum pension from a defined benefit scheme is two-thirds final (capped) salary. A lump-sum benefit of up to 2.25 times the maximum occupational pension, or 25 per cent of a personal pension fund, may be taken tax free.

There are specific anomalies and difficulties that arise from the multiplicity of tax codes and the complexities of individual tax codes. In the case of an occupational money-purchase scheme, for example, there is a contribution limit on the employee but not on the employer. Because there is no contribution limit on the employer there is a benefit limit that has to be administered and monitored. Meanwhile, AVC schemes have benefit limits that are considered in conjunction with the total benefit individuals will receive from the occupational schemes of which they are members. As a result of the multiplicity of systems, there are transfer regulations to limit occupational benefits being moved to personal schemes and possibly avoiding both contribution limits and benefit limits, and there are various sets of regulations that dictate the types of scheme of which an individual can be a member concurrently.

The Finance Act 2004 introduces simplified benefit rules from 2006 and reduces the number of systems.

The overall tax position

The overall effect of these tax rules in practice is complex:

- Subject to the limits, contributions made to approved schemes are generally fully exempt. Breach of the contribution limits could result in the scheme losing Inland Revenue approval and hence the regime for unapproved schemes applying. The first E is, therefore, for most employees, unqualified for approved schemes. Its administration can be complex, however (see also Part 3). The Finance Act 2004 will remove controls on contributions to a greater extent, thus it is reasonable to state, without qualification, that UK pension funds have, and will in the future have, tax-exempt contributions.

- The apparent exemption of investment income from tax is illusory. Some three-quarters of the average pension fund was invested in equities at the time dividend tax credits were withdrawn.[4] Equities are taxed at the relevant corporation tax rate. So, assuming an average corporation tax rate of 30 per cent and on income tax basic rate of 22 per cent, the current system of taxing investment returns could be regarded as T, or even T^+, by a basic-rate taxpayer.
- Typically, one quarter of benefits is taken in tax-free form, so the final T is partial.

Overall, therefore, the current system could best be described as $ETT^{partial}$ or $ET^+T^{partial}$ in comparison with the EET benchmark.

Higher-rate tax relief

Some commentators have suggested that higher-rate tax relief on contributions should be abolished. Reference was made to this in DSS (1998), as there had been speculation that the government

---

4   76 per cent according to the W.M. All Funds Universe, Quarter 2, 1997.

had been attracted to the idea. The Green Paper did not, however, express an intention to go ahead with any such abolition. Proposals to abolish higher-rate tax relief have been made by Le Grand and Agulnik (1998) and by Downing Street advisers (see, for example, the *Sunday Times*, 20 October 2002).

If higher-rate tax relief were abolished, it would produce a system of $E^{\text{lower rate}}T^{+}T^{\text{partial}}$. If, however, the intention is to restrict the benefit of deferring tax until retirement to the basic rate of tax by collecting the higher-rate tax up front, it would be necessary also to abolish the higher rate of tax on pension benefits. In other words, $E^{\text{lower rate}}T^{+}T^{\text{partial lower rate}}$ would be necessary to produce the desired effect! The abolition of higher-rate tax relief on its own would produce an entirely arbitrary tax system for pensions and unnecessarily complicate the savings decision. It would also be virtually impossible to administer. If tax relief were given only at the basic rate but pension benefits were then taxed at the higher rate, this would amount to double taxation (income from pensions would be taxed at the higher rate but relief on contributions would have been given only at the lower rate). If, however, pension benefits were taxed at the basic rate even for higher-rate taxpayers, it would create a tax system that would make our current quagmire look straightforward. Also, if tax relief were given only at the basic rate, there would be an incentive for higher-rate taxpayers to have their contributions made by their company (to avoid tax). No doubt the Inland Revenue would then want to class companies' pension contributions as a taxable benefit at the higher rate of tax.[5] This would lead to huge practical difficulties,

---

5   In fact, because of the difficulty of attributing employer contributions to employees in the case of defined benefit schemes, the proposals outlined in the *Sunday Times* (op. cit.) proposed exempting employer contributions to a scheme from

however, particularly for defined benefit schemes, the contributions of which are not attributable to individual members. Overall, proposals for the abolition of higher-rate tax relief have been insufficiently thought through, both from the point of view of public finance economics and their administration.

In summary, neither the current pension fund tax system, nor proposals to abolish higher-rate tax relief and move to $E^{\text{lower rate}}T+T^{\text{partial}}$, have any obvious economic rationale, unlike EET, TEE (the ISA regime) or TTE (the comprehensive income tax regime). The authors' preference is for a regime as close as possible to EET. This would mean establishing a method whereby returns to equities could be, as far as possible, tax free, but where there was no tax-free lump sum.

Costs of pension provision under different tax regimes

We have shown that, in principle, the tax system for pensions does not follow the ideal of an EET tax system. There is arbitrary taxation of equity returns within a pension fund and an arbitrary tax-free lump sum. In Appendix B we show how far away from EET the pension fund taxation system is in terms of the cost of financing a given pension, and illustrate how far the current tax system is from an economically coherent system. The results of the calculations in Appendix B are described below. In previously published work, Booth and Cooper (2002) show the impact of different tax regimes on pension levels achieved from defined contribution schemes with different tax arrangements. Here we

the abolition of higher-rate tax relief! Clearly such an approach is unsustainable and, as far as the Inland Revenue would be concerned, untenable.

concentrate on defined benefit schemes. We look at the cost of a given set of pension benefits, when the scheme faces four different tax regimes. The first tax regime is the existing regime, described above. The second regime is that which existed before the withdrawal of tax credits on UK equity dividends by Gordon Brown in 1997. The third is a comprehensive income tax system where contributions are made out of post-tax income and pension fund investment returns are taxed – in other words, as if pensions had all tax relief abolished. The final regime is a pure expenditure tax (so that the returns from equity investments are untaxed and all corporation tax paid on company equity returns is reclaimed).

Comparison of the cost of funding benefits under tax regimes

The results in Appendix B show that the removal of tax relief on dividends (moving from the pre-1997 to the post-1997 regime) should have increased the standard contribution rate of a typical pension scheme, to fund a given level of benefits, by 9 per cent. These results are consistent with those found for defined contribution schemes (see ibid.). A 9 per cent increase in pension fund contribution rates can be seen as the cost of that particular tax change to companies with defined benefit pension schemes.

The expenditure tax regime gives rise to the lowest cost of funding a pension benefit. This arises because investment returns, including equity returns, are fully tax free under this tax regime. If there were a pure expenditure tax regime, the standard contribution rate relative to the current (post-1997) regime would be reduced by 28 per cent. As expected, these results support the conclusion that the present tax system is a significant departure from the EET expenditure tax basis often quoted in the literature.

Pension funds are not nearly as favourably treated from a tax point of view as is often suggested to be the case.[6]

If there were a comprehensive income tax regime, the cost of funding benefits would increase by 14 per cent, after allowing for all tax considerations, compared with the cost of funding benefits under the current regime. This would represent the increased cost of pension provision from removing any special tax treatment of pensions, so that they were taxed just like other savings products. It should be noted that the increased cost would depend on the particular circumstances of a scheme and its members' salary profiles – the increased cost of 14 per cent represents the increased cost for a typical scheme.

Thus the post-1997 tax system leads to a contribution rate somewhat closer to that which would exist under a comprehensive income tax system than that which would exist if pension funds really did face an EET regime. Some of the so-called 'tax privileges' of pension saving are not as complete as is often suggested (for example, investment returns from equities are taxed at a rate even higher than the standard rate of income tax). On the other hand, some aspects of the tax position are better than would exist under an expenditure tax (for example, the tax-free lump sum). In fact, the tax system surrounding pension schemes is incoherent, encouraging the Inland Revenue to create a 'quagmire' in terms of the detailed application of the rules (see below and Part 3). In particular, the existence of the tax-free lump sum provides a potential area of tax avoidance and encourages the Inland

---

6   A further complication to the tax position of contributions arises because employers do not pay national insurance contributions on their contributions, whereas employee contributions to the scheme are paid net of both employer and employee NICs.

Revenue to develop anti-avoidance regulations. Further calculations show that, in terms of the cost of funding a given benefit, the benefit of the tax-free lump sum almost exactly offsets the cost of the tax paid on equity investments – this is an important finding, the implications of which will be discussed further in Part 3.

One aspect of the incoherence of the current pension fund tax regime is the differential treatment of equities compared with other investments. Bond returns, direct property returns and cash returns are totally tax free (thus following the logic of the expenditure tax system). Equity returns are taxed at 30 per cent. Property returns are not taxed unless property is held through property investment company shares, in which case it is taxed on the same basis as equity returns. Thus the tax position of a fund worsens the more investment takes place in equities (see Booth and Cooper, 2000; Emmerson and Tanner, 2000; Booth and Cooper, 2002).

Regulation and the tax system

In the section above we examined the economic basis of the tax treatment of pensions. Despite the fact that it was demonstrated that pensions do not follow the EET tax system commonly supposed, it is nevertheless true that their tax position is more favourable than that for most other savings vehicles.[7] It is therefore reasonable for the Inland Revenue to impose some limits on the extent to which the tax position of pensions can be exploited and some restrictions on the behaviour of those saving through pension schemes. We have indicated the reasons why pension

---

7   Although, for individuals on stable earnings, below the higher-rate tax band, there are situations in which the tax framework for pensions saving is not significantly better than that for ISAs: see Emmerson and Tanner (2000).

schemes should receive tax treatment that is close to EET. One of these reasons is to mitigate the economic distortions caused by the state offering means-tested benefits in retirement. One restriction that it is reasonable to put on individuals saving through pensions vehicles, therefore, is that pension funds should, in the first place, be used to purchase annuities.

Nevertheless, the current regulations limiting the use of pension vehicles are far more restrictive than is required by adherence to the principles enunciated above. The tax system is also far more complex, leading to paperwork costs as well as reducing choice and market transparency for pension scheme members. Indeed, the paperwork costs may be so high that they discourage a large number of people from pension saving altogether.

Annuity purchase rules, contribution and benefit limits

Currently, there are restrictions on the financial purposes to which a defined contribution pension fund can be put, and also restrictions on the annuity structure of defined benefit schemes. Furthermore, there are contribution limits on defined contribution schemes and benefit limits on defined benefit schemes. There are, then, complex rules dictating the relationship between defined benefit and defined contribution schemes. The current limits on contributions and benefits were described earlier in this chapter, although, as has been noted, these are in the process of being liberalised. The annuitisation rules strongly discourage, and in many circumstances prevent, less than 75 per cent of a pension fund (or equivalent in a defined benefit scheme) being used to purchase anything other than an annuity.

Annuitisation requirements restrict the freedom of individuals to manage their pension income in retirement as they see fit (particularly in a situation of declining health). They also lead to extra administrative costs for defined contribution occupational schemes and contracted-out personal pension schemes, as well as creating arbitrary inconsistencies between the different arrangements. The annuitisation rules also create risks from pension saving that do not exist in other forms of saving.

There are two main economic reasons for the regulations imposed by governments on the ways in which pension assets are used and the regulations limiting the amount of pension provision that can be made. These rules, it can be argued:

- prevent moral hazard (for example, prevent individuals spending all their retirement income savings at the point of retirement and then claiming means-tested benefits from the state); and
- prevent individuals from 'over-providing'. The rationale here is that pensions are tax privileged, to help people provide an annuity in old age and prevent them becoming a burden on the state. If people want to save more than for this basic requirement, they should use non-tax-privileged savings vehicles.

The tax qualification and annuitisation rules, as currently structured, are more geared towards the second point than the first. Many of the regulations were designed at a time when marginal rates of tax were much higher (up to 83 per cent) and so the value of up-front tax relief on contributions was, correspondingly, much higher. We have shown above that the tax system is no longer particularly favourable towards pension provision. If the tax-free lump sum were abolished (see Part 3), the Inland Revenue would have no need to take such interest in the form in which benefits are received. The first point made above about the annuitisation rules has, however, become more important than hitherto because of the extension of means testing. We suggest in Part 3 that a simple annuitisation rule be developed, for both defined benefit and defined contribution schemes, which addresses the moral hazard problem, and that most other rules surrounding the tax position of pension funds can be abolished.

11 THE PROBLEM OF UNFUNDED PENSIONS

While the issue of the unfunded pensions burden is not the main focus of this work, we provide a brief discussion of the issues here. Brown (1995) and Lunnon (1996) have suggested that there is macroeconomic equivalence between 'pay as you go' (PAYGO) pensions paid from taxes and funded schemes.[1] Their argument is that whether pension benefits are funded or not is irrelevant because all the people in a country can consume goods and services produced by today's workers only in aggregate, whether or not benefits are funded. Therefore the pensions paid to today's pensioners must come from the production of today's workers. This argument ignores the role that capital plays in the economy, something that is fundamental and basic in economics.

The person funding a pension establishes a capital fund that provides property rights over future returns on investment. This is a fundamentally different system from PAYGO pensions, where pensions for today's pensioners are financed by taxes from today's taxpayers. There is no effort in a PAYGO system to build up a fund or secure property rights on future investment returns.

---

1   Many other authors have too, although mainly non-economists, often writing papers for trade bodies, professional magazine articles, etc. We cite these two authors for having sparked a major debate on this subject within the actuarial profession. There are some subtle arguments that can justify the equivalence argument – see below.

This represents a fundamental reason for preferring private to state pension provision right across the income scale. As has been noted, one author does not fully accept this perspective, and our proposals allow choice, at the individual level, between state and private provision through the mechanism of contracting out in respect of the basic level of pension provision.

It could, however, be argued that private, funded pension saving might substitute for other forms of saving rather than lead to new saving, so that there is no new capital formation from pensions saving; indeed, we use this argument below in the discussion of compulsory pension provision. Also, the development of PAYGO pensions debts might lead to increased saving as individuals seek to meet the perceived increase in the future burden of taxation necessary to pay for state pensions in the future (this is known as 'Ricardian equivalence'). In both these cases, there may be no net change in aggregate saving from private pension provision. The privately funded pensions themselves, however, are secured by property rights on returns from future investment, and so, at a microeconomic level, give individual savers a claim on the returns from the investments financed by their pension saving. If an increase in aggregate saving were to take place in response to the extension of a PAYGO system, under the Ricardian equivalence argument, it would not secure a pension benefit for any individual.

There are circumstances in which so-called PAYGO pensions could be regarded as funded because the income from contributions is effectively a substitute for issuing government debt (Minford, 1998). Some economists would therefore regard PAYGO pensions as funded by implicit government debt and PAYGO pension liabilities as an extension of government debt.

Booth (1998) discusses this issue in much greater detail and concludes that such analogies are valid, but only up to a point and only in respect of certain types of unfunded schemes. It is certainly true that a state pension based on an accruals system that allows contracting out should have a greater degree of security than a citizen's pension (see Introduction) and could be regarded as being funded by government debt. Indeed, the authors would argue that government accounting systems should account for such state pension liabilities (see below).

The OECD has calculated the implicit government debt associated with PAYGO social insurance schemes in the developed world. Demographic changes that give rise to these debts and the policy issues that result have been discussed by authors such as Kessler (1996) and Chand and Jaeger (1996), and the arguments have been summarised in Booth and Dickinson (1997). There are several ways of quantifying the accumulated social security obligations. The OECD (reported in Paribas, 1995, and discussed in Stein, 1997, and, more recently, in Daykin, 2002) looked at long-term budget deficits and national debt figures for various countries. The estimates were based on the assumption that 1995 policies would continue. By 2030, Germany was projected to have a budget deficit of 9 per cent of GDP and a debt-to-GDP ratio of over 100 per cent caused by unfunded pensions costs. Figures for France were similar. Italy was projected to have a budget deficit of 13 per cent and a debt-to-GDP ratio of 120 per cent. The UK, with its low level of state pension provision, had a projected budget surplus and a projected debt-to-GDP ratio of below 10 per cent. Policy in the UK has changed considerably since these figures were calculated, so whether the UK can maintain and, indeed, has maintained such a low level of implicit debt is questionable (Cooper et al., 2003).

Future state pension liabilities are often expressed as a percentage of GDP. If the state actually intends to pay the future pensions, these liabilities are the equivalent of government debt that is not financed by assets held. It would be reasonable to add pension liabilities to official government debt when comparing national debt figures across countries. An official quantification of the level of unfunded pension liabilities would provide useful information for voters, for whom information about the cost of future pension liabilities is extremely opaque.

Changes in population structure can give rise to problems in relation to funded schemes as well as for PAYGO schemes. For example, when a population ages there will be changes in asset prices, rates of return and wages. These are price signals indicating changes in the relative scarcity and abundance of labour and capital. If a market-based system of funded pensions is to work effectively, it is important that individuals are able to react to such price signals. Reactions might include increasing (or decreasing) saving, investing overseas or extending the working life (which would be a rational reaction to both labour scarcity and capital abundance). The encroachment of a system of means-tested benefits, with benefits increasing in level at a given age (the state pension age), removes some of the flexibility that needs to exist in a funded pensions system if it is to respond to changing demographic profiles. We discuss potential solutions to these problems and ways to make funded pensions respond to price signals more effectively in Part 3.

Given the fundamental difference between funded and unfunded pensions, it would seem reasonable for the government not to act in a way that would lead to a reduction in funded pension provision. Indeed, as has been noted, the government has increasing funded pension provision as a stated objective. Recent policy, however, is likely to lead to the opposite happening – a reduction in funded pension provision in the long run. The recent Pensions Commission report (autumn 2004) provides plenty of evidence of the decline of private pension provision. The issue of whether pension provision should be funded or unfunded is one that has tended to divide those who believe in market solutions to economic problems from those who do not. This division should not be clear cut, however. It is possible to have state-provided funded pension provision, state-regulated funded provision or to intervene in other ways to ensure that (for example) the low paid receive help in developing funded pension provision. Thus it is possible to have a pension system with a significant degree of state intervention but with funded provision. It is also possible to have a private PAYGO system based on extended family or paternalistic company arrangements.

Notwithstanding these points, significant unfunded *state* pension debts do undermine economic freedom by imposing an implicit contractual burden on individuals who were not party to a free contract (see Booth, 1999, for a more detailed discussion of this). The coming generations of voters will have to finance pensions they have had no part in agreeing to. The proposals in Part 3 will increase the level of funded pensions and will work with the grain of the market and the price system in other respects. As has been discussed in the Introduction and is further discussed in Part 3, the particular state mechanism that we propose does impose discipline on the current generation of workers not to promise themselves benefits that they are unwilling to finance themselves, as a cohort.

Part 3
The Way Out of the Quagmire

Our principles for reform have been enunciated in the Introduction. We restate them briefly here.

- There may be a legitimate role for the government in providing a single means-tested benefit in retirement to act as a safety net: there is no reason, however, for the characteristics of that benefit to differ from the characteristics of means-tested benefits before retirement.
- The tax system for elderly people should be no different from that for younger people.
- There is an economic case for the state to require a particular minimum level of compulsory pension provision but that should not be greater than it is currently.
- Pension saving should remain outside the tax system until pension income is received.
- There should be no arbitrary benefits given to those who save for a pension (for example, a tax-free lump sum) and no arbitrary taxes on pension fund investments (for example, the taxation of equity returns while other investments are tax free).
- Given that pension saving should take place outside the tax system until benefits are received, it is reasonable for the

Inland Revenue to place some limits on provision, but such limits need not be onerous.

- The regulation of the solvency and funding of pension schemes should be limited to those parts of schemes that are designed to provide the minimum required compulsory provision.
- The pension system should not institutionalise a particular retirement age.

Most of this part is devoted to suggested reforms to the pension system. As there is so much support for increased compulsion, however, the authors felt that it was important to start Part 3 with a chapter explaining the reasons why they reject that approach.

12 EVALUATION OF PROPOSALS FOR MORE COMPULSION

One obvious way to deal with the serious disincentive problems caused by the interaction of the means-tested benefit system with the tax system, which has been described above in Parts 1 and 2, would be to have more compulsory pension provision. If the level of compulsory pension provision were greater than the level of means-tested benefits, means-tested benefits would cease to be an important disincentive. A number of commentators have suggested greater compulsory pension provision as a way of removing what is, in effect, a form of moral hazard caused by the extent of means testing. The most notable proponent of this approach is Frank Field (see, for example, Field in Deacon, 2002). Field also believes that greater compulsory pension provision would help ensure that everybody would contribute to their future pension and that it could be combined with greater income redistribution, thus strengthening, as Field would put it, social cohesion.

We reject proposals for increasing compulsory pension provision as this is attacking the symptoms of the problem of lack of pension provision (disincentives to save) rather than the causes (the growth of means-tested benefits) and therefore does not resolve the underlying problem. It immediately raises the issue of how the less well off could afford increased compulsory pension provision (see Booth in ibid.). Equally, if the less well off were enabled to afford increased pension provision through higher taxes used to redistribute income or through redistribution within the pension system, this would replace means testing in retirement with means testing during working years or higher explicit or implicit taxes. This would not necessarily resolve a moral hazard or disincentives problem: it would merely transfer it to a different part of the lifespan.

We noted at the end of Chapter 7 that the current level of compulsory pension provision (effectively the BSP plus S2P) was greater than the level of means-tested benefits. Current retirees often had a lower level of compulsory pension provision during their working lives, however, so they suffer from disincentives problems because the pension they receive may well be less than means-tested benefit levels. Current workers, despite the increased compulsory pension provision, have been led to expect a considerable extension of means-tested benefits through the linking of means-tested benefit levels to increases in earnings, while the BSP is linked only to prices. Thus current workers, making their decisions on the basis of expectations of future policy, also have their incentives eroded. *In developing any proposals, it is important not to neglect that individuals' behaviour will respond not to the system as it is at present but to their expectations of its development.*

Two main economic arguments can be advanced for greater compulsory pension provision. The first is based on what is often described as 'investor myopia'. If people are left to be responsible for their own pension arrangements, they may not save enough to provide an adequate pension because they will put short-term needs ahead of long-term saving. This argument, in effect, suggests that a pension is a 'merit good', the provision of which should be made compulsory, financed or subsidised by the state, because, left to their own devices, individuals will not make sufficient provision for their needs. Acceptance of this argument implies that under-saving can be expected to increase as occupational pensions decline and people rely more on personal pension schemes, since employers usually make significantly higher contributions to the former.

The second argument in favour of greater compulsory pension provision is based on the economic principles of 'second best'. If the merit good argument is not accepted, it could be assumed that, in the absence of government intervention, individuals would provide themselves with the optimum amount of pension provision. Governments, however, provide means-tested benefits that, as has been demonstrated above, distort savings incentives. This creates a 'second best' situation where there is an incentive for individuals to 'under-provide' for their pension needs. Nevertheless, the social benefits of more pension provision are greater than the private benefits because, if an individual increases pension saving, this reduces the cost to others of providing means-tested benefits.

One possible solution is for the state to provide incentives for individuals to save more for a pension than they would otherwise choose to provide for themselves – for example, by providing incentives through the tax system. Alternatively, a direct subsidy for pension provision could be given to those who are most likely to be at risk from disincentives arising from means-tested benefit provision.[1] Some would argue that if these strategies were

1   Le Grand and Agulnik (1998) argue that the current tax treatment of pensions in the UK provides an implicit subsidy for pension provision and express a preference for an explicit subsidy. It was not, however, the intention of those who designed the current tax system that it should form an implicit subsidy (see Part 2). Neil Collins, City Editor of the *Telegraph*, is a vocal proponent of explicit subsidy for pension provision using the 'BOGOF' (buy one get one free) approach.

ineffective in counteracting the disincentives to provide pensions that arise because of means-tested benefit provision, greater compulsory pension provision would be desirable. The government's Pensions Commission under Adair Turner is investigating these issues.

Arguments for compulsory pension provision have been well rehearsed in policy discussions on pensions issues. For example, the government consultation document, *Stakeholder Pensions* (published in 1997), said that 'a significant number of responses to the Pension Review urged an extension of compulsion'. Commentators on the issue often cite foreign examples. Both the Australian and Chilean pension systems (see Knox, 1998; Pinera, 1998) involve significant compulsory provision.

The debate about compulsory pension provision in the UK often appears to take place on the assumption that there is no compulsory provision at the moment. In fact, all employed and self-employed people with incomes greater than the lower earnings limit are de facto compelled to be in the government's basic state pension scheme and many others receive credits in the system. This implies the compulsory provision of a pension benefit of £4,139 p.a. (for someone credited with a full working lifetime). The cost of providing this benefit is equivalent to saving over £1,000 per annum (indexed to prices) throughout a working lifetime. Employed people have further compulsory provision through SERPS/S2P (or an equivalent or better private scheme for those who have contracted out of the state scheme), which targets at least 20 per cent of revalued career-average pay between the lower and upper earnings limits (see Part 1 for a description of SERPS/S2P). Many people now receive credits within this scheme too.

Figure 8   Interaction between Pension Credit and S2P

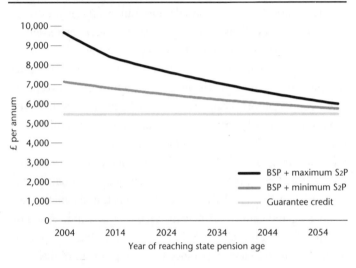

Someone retiring now with a full NIC record, having received median earnings (£20,400 p.a.) throughout their working lifetime, would receive a state pension of over £7,000, a replacement ratio of about one third, from age 65 (earlier for women). Compulsory provision above this level could be seen by some as penal.

Figure 8 shows the target state pension benefit under a mature S2P in real earnings terms, relative to the single person's guarantee credit part of the Pension Credit. It demonstrates how the replacement rate achievable from state pensions falls each year if the BSP continues to be increased no faster than prices and, as proposed, the single person's guarantee credit increases in line with average earnings.

There are a number of points that can be made related to

Figure 8. First, it is clear that the minimum compulsory provision is not less than the proposed minimum income guarantee for another 64 years! Thus, in theory, means-tested benefits should not impact, even on new entrants into the workforce, for another 24 years. This would seem to suggest that proposals for greater compulsory pension provision are not appropriate except on merit good grounds. There are some qualifying factors, however. First, there are still very high marginal rates of tax and benefit withdrawal (see Part 2) up to a much higher level of income when one considers the full Pension Credit scheme, which provides means-tested benefits up to income levels of approximately £144 per week in 2004/5 and also non-cash means-tested benefits such as housing and council tax benefit. Second, many individuals do not qualify for a full BSP or S2P. Nevertheless, this does put the moral hazard problem in perspective. The problem of disincentives caused by means testing would perhaps not be insurmountable if other policies were to be changed while leaving the level of compulsory provision broadly unchanged. The reasons why we would prefer there to be no significant change in the amount of compulsory pension provision are given below.

Reasons for not increasing compulsory pension provision

A number of reasons can be put forward which suggest that an increase in compulsory pension provision would not be the 'cure-all' that is sometimes suggested.

- The most direct way of addressing the specific moral hazard problem would be to extend the flat-rate part of compulsory, contributory, pension provision (see, for example, O'Connell, 2004[2]; Simpson, 2003). If this were done, then those who would see the greatest proportionate increase in their pension provision would be the lower paid, who may already be on means-tested benefits whilst of working age. Such means-tested benefits may have to be increased to help the low paid meet the increased national insurance or private pensions contributions. Means-tested benefits in retirement would then simply be replaced by increased means-tested benefits in work.

- Most individuals and families have significant debt during their early to mid working lives (mortgages, bank loans, and so on). It would be difficult to argue that greater pension provision is a sensible financial decision for such people. They would, in effect, be borrowing from one institution and lending to (saving with) another, with considerable transactions costs through interest spreads, product charges, and so on. Compulsory pension provision would, in effect, be making pensions mis-selling compulsory.

- A second-best economic position, caused by means-tested benefits altering the price of pension per unit of net (of benefit) pension received, can always be corrected more effectively via the price mechanism than by compulsion. The price mechanism can involve the provision of tax breaks or subsidies for pension provision. Other authors, such as Neil Collins and Le Grand and Agulnik, have suggested providing an explicit subsidy for pension provision. We also reject

---

2   Various different ways of financing an extension were discussed by O'Connell. Her analysis was based on implementing the scheme used in New Zealand.

their approaches, however, as they would add further to the complexity of the system.

- Pension provision could lead savers to substitute pension savings for other savings with savers replacing flexible savings vehicles with less flexible (compulsory) savings vehicles, less able to meet individual needs. This could create a welfare loss, particularly for those with impaired health who may not expect to live sufficiently long to receive a pension or who would receive a pension for a shorter than average time.

- Similarly, savers could simply increase their financial liabilities, which they would then plan to repay using their pension assets. For example, they could choose to continue their mortgage into retirement and repay their mortgage using their pension (or repay it on retirement using the lump-sum benefit). Again, this leads to savers incurring the intermediation costs of both borrowing and saving. The only way the government could prevent this from happening would be to increase the level of control of all financial decisions taken by individuals.

- Individuals may prefer to be supported in old age from the proceeds of working beyond traditional retirement age, from the income or capital from non-financial assets (for example, by letting property or 'downsizing') or, in many cultures, through extended family networks. Greater compulsory pension provision institutionalises a particular form of retirement provision.

Given that the economic case for greater compulsion is weak and there are a number of arguments against greater compulsion, the authors would argue that greater compulsory pension provision (whether private compulsory pension provision as in Australia or Chile or state compulsory pension provision as in many EU countries) should not be required in the UK.

Other arguments have been put forward for compulsion – for example, that compulsion will raise the savings ratio, helping the economy as a whole, and also lower the unit cost of pension provision.[3] These arguments are of a fundamentally different character from the moral hazard argument. Compulsory provision of any product may lower unit cost in the short term. In the long term, however, this is at the expense of innovation and consumer efficiency, and could lead to uncompetitive market practices.

With regard to the savings ratio argument, we believe that it should be up to individuals to determine their own consumption patterns, bearing in mind their own time preferences and desired returns to capital. Given current returns to capital, savers might choose to save less because this is optimal for them. Increased saving would finance an increase in the capital that provides the return to the saver, and establish a property right on the returns from that capital, which increases the individual's pension. It is not clear how it helps the economy as a whole, however. Rather, it could do the reverse, since a big pool of compulsory savings could lower the productivity of capital.

Others have proposed greater compulsory pension provision as part of the development of a wider pensions system, based on defined benefits, guaranteed by the state (for example, Field in Deacon, 2002). A feature of these systems is that all contributors pay higher contributions, as a percentage of salary, than the

---

3   Indeed, the document *Stakeholder Pensions*, published in 1997, says that many of those who proposed greater compulsory pension provision did so because they believed that it would reduce the unit cost of provision.

current compulsory equivalent, and there is then redistribution within the system so that the less well off receive a pension that is better than 'actuarially fair', given their contribution record. In effect, the well off are paying higher compulsory contributions to finance pensions for the less well off: this is not unlike the current BSP system except that the proposals often involve greater private sector involvement (for example, in the investment of funds). As well as leading to greater compulsory provision overall, Field's proposals would have involved the replacement and/or supplementing of tax-financed redistribution with income redistribution through a pension scheme. In economic terms, this is little different from increasing taxes on higher-paid groups to finance greater means-tested payments to lower-paid groups.

Thus, we reject reform that is based on increasing the extent of compulsory pension provision. Although the current state pension system and its interaction with the private sector is far from straightforward, it does involve a compulsory element that is sufficient to address the moral hazard problem were it not for the existence of other policies which, themselves, should be addressed.

13 SOCIAL SECURITY BENEFITS AND STATE PENSIONS

Non-cash, non-means-tested benefits

The government has recently introduced two non-cash but non-means-tested social security benefits that are age dependent. The first is the winter fuel allowance, which, although presented as a non-cash benefit, is a cash benefit in practice. It is paid on a 'per-household' basis, when one member of the household reaches age 60, but is independent of heating needs, climate or actual fuel consumed (pensioners who live in Spain during the winter are eligible, as well as those who live in Aberdeen). This benefit does not impair economic efficiency in an obvious way (it is paid to workers aged over 60 as well as to the retired) but is of no obvious benefit either. It adds to the complexity of the system as a whole, is costly to pay out and to claim, and has to be collected in taxes before then being paid out as a social security payment. We propose it should be abolished.

The second benefit is a genuine non-cash benefit – a free colour television licence is available to any household where one member is over the age of 70. This benefit is paid on a per-household basis and does not influence taxable income or means-tested benefits. Individuals who do not own a television set (perhaps because they are blind) or who are in communal housing (where individual television licences do not have to be purchased) receive no benefit.

It is difficult to suggest any economic rationale for free television licences; it surely cannot be argued that a colour television is a merit good. Any economic or social objective (for example, giving more assistance to the less well off) could be achieved more efficiently in a different way. We also propose that this benefit be abolished.

Means-tested benefits, social security minimum income and the level of compulsory pension provision

Economists could make a major contribution to pension policy if they could persuade the government to revise the relative levels of means-tested benefits and compulsory pension provision to avoid the moral hazard problems that we have described. The political process should be left to determine the level at which means-tested benefits should be set. In 2002 Age Concern believed that £160 per week was the minimum income needed for subsistence (Parker, 2002), and this would vary depending on the size of household and other factors. We do not make any further comment on the size of the basic means-tested benefit that should be paid to individuals or households – that is a political decision. Parker notwithstanding, however, the means-tested benefit should not vary with age. Needs-contingent, but not age-contingent, benefits can be paid if necessary.

If the level of compulsory pension provision is driven by the one consideration of removing the moral hazard to remain on means-tested benefits, then many of the other problems with the pensions system, particularly those imposed by government regulation, can be addressed.

Income support and means-tested benefits

If compulsory pension provision is sufficient to prevent most people from entering the means-tested benefit net, it might be thought that means-tested benefits and the various taper provisions would not be necessary. Even in the long term, however, when a system is fully mature, there will always be some people who have avoided 'compulsory' pension provision: while the system may be 'compulsory' it may not be quite universal, even if credits are given to people who care for their elderly, bring up their children, etc. Also, some people who have contracted out of the state system may have a smaller pension than the 'compulsory minimum' as a result of poor investment decisions. Nevertheless, the various mechanisms to provide credits towards compulsory pension provision will ensure that most people will have incomes in excess of income support, at least in the long term, but taper provisions will still be necessary to ensure that a relatively small number of individuals, who have somehow managed to avoid compulsory pension provision and qualify for income support, still have incentives to save and work. Such tapers might also be necessary to provide incentives to individuals to invest pension savings in a prudent way.[1]

The current government expresses an 'intention' regarding the setting of future means-tested benefit levels. This is not set in legislation but nevertheless is important in influencing expectations. We propose that the government's intention with regard to the future level of means-tested benefits should be expressed as follows:

---

1   We do not pursue this issue further except to note that the authors would prefer a taper in the means-tested benefits system to investment regulation to provide the appropriate incentives for individuals to invest prudently. A price signal is better than direct control.

> The level of means-tested benefits will generally increase
> in line with the price level. Additional increases may be
> given, but, except in extraordinary circumstances, these
> increases will not be greater than the rate at which the level
> of compulsory pension provision is increasing. The objective
> will be to maintain the minimum means-tested benefit
> payment around subsistence level in the long term.

Council tax and housing benefits could remain with their current taper levels. There are good arguments for turning these benefits into cash benefits, but these are beyond the scope of this paper.

A new state pension

We define a new state pension benefit, earned on an accruals basis, as follows. For each year for which an employee has a national insurance record of any type, or receives home responsibility protection or otherwise receives credits in the state pension system, a pension is accrued as follows:

$$\text{Pension received at retirement} = \frac{1}{45} \times 8{,}500 \times (1 + g)^{70 - t}$$

where g is a rate of growth of the accrued pension between the age of accrual t and the 'state pension reference age', which we believe should be set at age 70. g is fixed at a level between the rate of growth of retail prices and the rate of growth of earnings.[2]

---

2   For example, g could be halfway between the rates of growth of earnings and prices, or the rate of growth of prices plus 1 per cent. To some extent it is a political matter to determine g. Although g could be changed for future years' accrued pension, to change g after a given year's pension had accrued would cause

The maximum number of years of accrual would be 45. The pension received at retirement would be index-linked to prices. This formula would ensure that the state pension decreased as a proportion of average gross earnings but, owing to the method of up-rating, would provide a partly earnings-related benefit that could complement individual saving.

In real terms, this pension is broadly equal in amount to the sum of the current BSP and S2P (when – or if – S2P is capped), up-rated at less than the level one would expect under S2P but more than the level one would expect under the BSP. It is also broadly equivalent, in cost terms, to the current level of the BSP: a higher pension than the current level of BSP would be received but from a later age. The figure chosen for the full level of pension, however, is intended to be illustrative. As has been noted, it is a matter for Parliament to decide the level of subsistence means-tested benefit and hence the level of pension.

An actuarially adjusted pension could also be received from any age between 60 and 70, as long as the pensioner could demonstrate that insured annuities, including the state pension, were being received at least equal to 1.5 times the level of means-tested benefits: this provision would ensure that the individual did not become a burden on the state by retiring early but would otherwise be a liberalising measure. Otherwise, the pension would start to be paid from age 70 or later. Again, an actuarially adjusted pension could be received if the individual elected to start to receive the pension after age 70.

---

inequity between people who had contracted out and those who had not. Within the current system, in so far as comparisons can be made between the current system and our proposed framework, g is the increase in RPI for the basic state pension and the increase in average earnings for S2P.

This pension would replace the BSP and S2P. It would be as easy to administer as S2P will be, after stage two of the reform, when it is proposed that S2P will become flat rate. There would be only one pension to administer, however, not two. It should be easy to provide individuals with statements, illustrating pension projections. There would be a considerable amount of certainty regarding the real amount of pension that would be received by any individual. It would then be relatively easy for individuals to make decisions regarding how much additional pension provision should be made.

The system would work on an accruals basis, similar to flat-rate S2P. This means that, once an individual had worked a given year, a sum of pension, determined by the formula above, would come as close as is possible in the relationship between the individual and the state pension system to a 'contractual right'. This is important to ensure the integrity of contracting-out systems and to protect the pension from political meddling.[3] It would make it much more difficult for the government to reduce benefits that had been previously accrued. But, likewise, voters would not be able to vote themselves increases in pensions for past years of accrual – they would be able to increase the level of pensions only for future years of accrual, and they would have to pay for this through higher NICs. This is an important aspect of the political economy of the system (see Chapters 1 and 17).

There is a potential problem that could arise from this

---

3   It could be argued that a corporation, along the lines of the student loan company, should be set up to administer this whole system, and that state pensions be notionally (or even explicitly) invested in government bonds and that future state pension liabilities should be published. All of these would make the system less amenable to political meddling.

approach – and this problem has, indeed, arisen in the SERPS/ S2P system. What would happen if a government wanted to change the basis of future accrual of pensions – for example, change the age at which the basic level of the state pension would be paid to 71 while keeping the amount of pension accrued each year the same? For future years of accrual, there would be no difficulty – pension would be accrued that would be received at age 71. But an individual who had already accrued some pension to be received at age 70 would face the very complexity we are trying to avoid. That individual could, for example, accrue £70 per week of pension to be received from age 70 and £70 to be received from age 71 if a change to the BSP age were made in the middle of his working life. This situation could be sorted out at retirement, given proposals we have made for flexible BSP ages, but perhaps only actuaries would then understand their state pension position! We propose a simple way of dealing with this problem, through an Independent Pensions Commission, described below (see page 151).

Contracting out and pension scheme regulation

The proposals we make below will allow anybody to be a member of an occupational defined benefit scheme and a personal or stakeholder scheme simultaneously.[4] As is currently the case, contracting out of the new state pension should be allowed on a defined benefit or a defined contribution basis so that those who wish to make appropriate private pension

---

4   The simplification proposals announced by the Inland Revenue also permit 'con-currency'.

arrangements do not have to belong to the state pension scheme and will receive an appropriate refund of NICs or will pay a reduced NIC rate.

If an individual is a member of an occupational scheme that is contracted out, members and/or their employers will pay an appropriately reduced rate of NIC, as is currently the case – although it could be argued that the current level of contracted-out national insurance reduction is too low.

Individuals who wish to contract out of the state pension scheme on a defined contribution basis will be able to do so too. Members of schemes that are not contracted out (as well as people who are not members of occupational schemes) would be able to contract out of the compulsory minimum state pension on a defined contribution basis and receive an actuarially neutral, age-related national insurance rebate to invest in a personal pension scheme. The economic logic of the contracting-out system is that the actuarial cost of accruing the state benefit should be returned to any individual who chooses to contract out of the state scheme and make personal provision. National insurance rebates equal to the actuarial value of the pension benefit forgone by leaving the state scheme would be paid to any individual who contracted out, including those in receipt of home responsibility protection.[5] These proposals would achieve a significant increase in the potential to contract out, by allowing individuals to contract out of all state pension provision and by allowing all individuals, even those who do not pay NICs, who accrue an entitlement to a state

---

5   We make no comment on who should be eligible for home responsibility protection (the accrual of state pension rights without any contributions being made) – again, this is a political matter for Parliament to decide.

pension to contract out and receive a payment into a personal pension scheme.[6]

It is possible that fewer occupational schemes will wish to contract out, particularly as our proposals for regulation with regard to benefits above basic compulsory levels are very liberal – schemes may wish only to provide benefits above state pension levels. Members of occupational schemes that have not contracted out, however, will be able to contract out easily, at an individual level, if they wish to. Occupational schemes could then concentrate on providing some sort of earnings-related benefit above the basic level of provision, free from oppressive regulation.

With regard to regulation, we should go back to first principles and ask, 'Why do we regulate pension schemes?' Two reasons could be justified from economic principles. Where pension funds are contracted out of the state scheme, it is reasonable for the government to impose regulations to ensure that the scheme can meet the benefits individuals would otherwise have obtained from the state. Otherwise, the state would be providing national insurance rebates to people who did not have appropriate, alternative private provision. Second, it could be argued that there is 'asymmetric information' in the process of the provision of complex pension products: the employee knows less about the operation of the pension fund than the employer or provider, or the purchaser knows less about the product than the seller. Various mechanisms have evolved in the market to

---

6   It is arguable that the change should be retrospective, so that individuals who have accumulated accrued state pension entitlements can receive a transfer payment into an appropriate scheme. The privatisation of government pension liabilities could be regarded as equally important to the development of a market economy as was the privatisation of state assets.

deal with these problems (for example, the trustee system in occupational schemes).

The application of these two principles, however, justifies a much lighter regulatory burden than exists currently, but whether a scheme is contracted out will influence the degree of regulation. The following approach to regulation should be taken:

- The scheme would have to demonstrate that it had the funds to meet an expected pension liability for all members equal to the benefit members would have accrued in the state scheme for any time those members have been contracted out of the state scheme. The basis for determining that the scheme was sufficiently well funded to meet these benefits would be based on the principles set out in guidance on funding defined benefit schemes at buy-out cost published by the actuarial profession.[7] These benefits and pensions in payment relating to minimum compulsory provision would have priority over all other benefits in a winding up – this is contrary to the position under the 1995 Pensions Act, which gave priority to pensions in payment above all other obligations. The national insurance rebates provided to members and employers in defined benefit schemes should reflect the strong solvency standards that are expected.
- Any transfer values under defined benefit schemes in relation to contracted-out benefits should both be given and received calculated on the GN 9 basis.

---

7   Guidance Note 9 (GN 9).

The few other regulations relating to an occupational scheme would ensure that:

- boards of trustees are constructed in a way such that members' interests are properly represented and will be paramount when decisions relating to the scheme are taken;
- the investment policy and funding policy are well publicised;
- the arrangements for priority on winding up and the transfer of benefits are made clear to all members;
- the funding level in relation to the non-compulsory minimum pension benefits that the scheme provides is well publicised, as are the basis on which the funding strategy is calculated and the underlying risks inherent in the funding and investment strategy.

Professions, trade bodies, trade unions, trustees and so on could be encouraged to cooperate to develop some standard approaches that schemes could follow when managing transfer values, benefit accrual and winding-up procedures, and explain the risks of different approaches in order to help improve public understanding. It should be the role of private sector bodies such as trade unions, after taking professional advice, to monitor the solvency of their members' schemes.

Under these proposals, minimum levels of pensions would be more secure than currently (although the regulations designed to ensure security would be much less complex). Contracting-out requirements would be much less onerous. All other regulation of defined benefit pension schemes would be considerably reduced. It is arguable that benefits that do not relate to contracting out will be less secure than under current regulation. The rules relating to the security of such benefits, however, will be better understood and more transparent. Those members who were concerned about the security of pension benefits would understand the structures that determined their security and could decide how much independent saving to make.

There would be some simple issues for schemes to determine. For example, given that benefits relating to the minimum compulsory provision would take priority over all other benefits, individuals could be at risk of losing benefits in payment after retirement if a scheme were to become insolvent – something that rarely happens now. It would be incumbent on employees and their representatives to consider very basic risk management issues if they wanted to be protected from such eventualities. Such issues are probably fairly straightforward and relate to questions such as: What is the funding level of the scheme? What is the investment policy? Are annuities in payment insured? Very often regulation can obscure rather than help risk management processes.

If a scheme does not contract out, the only regulations that need apply to it are those relating to transparency and information provision.

Under these proposals, the government's proposed Pension Protection Fund, to protect accrued rights in occupational pensions schemes, would not be formed. Schemes could make their own benefit insurance arrangements if they chose to do so. We have proposed a strong solvency standard for benefits in contracted-out schemes in respect of those benefits that replace the state pension. There is of course a risk that, despite the strong solvency standard, a scheme might suffer some kind of financial loss that would undermine those benefits. There are also risks attached to state pensions and to defined contribution benefits.

It is not clear that all risks can or should be eliminated from the provision even of the most basic pension benefits.

Transition arrangements

The principles on which the above proposals are based are durable. The objectives of the proposed regulations are straightforward and have economic merit, so it should not be necessary to continually change the rules under which pension schemes operate. Continual rule changes and several 'layers' of benefits accrued under different rules were two of the issues identified in Pickering (2002) which have led to considerable increases in the costs of operating defined benefit schemes.

The simplicity of the proposed system of state pension provision is such that it would be possible to apply it retrospectively to avoid the problems that Pickering identified. Individuals could have accrual in the new state scheme awarded to them to reflect the SERPS and S2P that they have accrued to date and the BSP they have notionally accrued. Future years of accrual would be awarded in the new system. Existing administrative systems would be able to handle such an approach. The terms for handling the transfer of existing pension benefit into pension benefits under the proposed new system could be handled by the Independent Pensions Commission (see the next section).

An Independent Pensions Commission

We propose that there should be an Independent Pensions Commission (IPC) set up to take certain decisions in relation to the state pension scheme which are technical, rather than political. There are two issues identified below which the IPC could deal with, in addition to problems related to the transition from the existing to a new state pension system (see the previous section).

Whenever the government makes a change to the state pension which involves a change in the age at which future accrued state pension will be received, in order to avoid complexity the pension that has been accrued so far by individuals should be received from the new retirement age. If, however, the retirement age were increased, for example, this would involve an effective reduction in state pension benefits already accrued and undermine the accruals system on which we believe the state pension should be based. This is best illustrated by an example. A person aged 50 might have accrued a pension of £100 per week, in the state pension system, to be paid from age 70. The government might then wish to increase the state pension age to (say) 71, and that individual might expect to accrue a further £35 a week to be received from that age. It is cumbersome and complex for an individual to have different entitlements at different ages in this way, and it would not be fair if the government suddenly announced an increase in the age from which previously accrued state pension would be paid. We propose that, in these circumstances, individuals have their accrued entitlements up-rated so that the actuarial value of the up-rated pension, received from the new retirement age, is equal to the actuarial value of the pension so far accrued. Such calculations are not complex and are carried out routinely by insurance companies when policies are adjusted. Such an approach would allow the government to make changes to the state pension scheme that were not retrospective but took immediate effect for newly accrued pension. Members of the state pension scheme would still have one pension paid from a specific age.

We propose that, when the government has decided to change key aspects of the state benefit, such as the state pension age, the IPC should recommend to Parliament enhancements to accrued pensions. The IPC would be made up entirely of non-government employees but it could take advice from the Government Actuary and any private sector experts. Recommendations would have to be overruled by a specific decision of Parliament. The IPC would leave political decisions (for example, the level of pensions and retirement ages) to the government.

When a change is made to the state pension scheme, individuals would receive a letter saying words to the effect that:

> The government has decided that your contributions to
> the state pension from next year onwards will lead to a
> pension of £x per week for every year of contributions
> you make to be received from age 71, rather than from
> age 70 as at present. In accordance with legislation, the
> IPC has, in order to ensure that your benefits are clearly
> understood and simple to administer, decided to increase
> the pension to which your contributions to date have
> entitled you from £50 to £55, to be paid from age 71.
> This increased pension benefit reflects the fact that the
> pension you have accrued so far will be received a year
> later than you expected at the time it was accrued. These
> amounts are up-rated before retirement in accordance
> with the legislation and up-rated after retirement in line
> with the retail price index. You may still take a pension
> from age 70 if you wish but it will be adjusted to allow
> for the earlier payment.

The IPC would act rather like the trustees of a private pension scheme. The IPC's decisions could be challenged in the courts if it did not adhere to its role as laid out in legislation.

The IPC should also set recommendations for contracting out national insurance rebates that could be overruled only by a specific decision of Parliament. These rebates should reflect, as near as is possible, the cost of the pension benefit that is forgone by an individual of a particular age who contracts out of the state pension scheme.

Benefits of the above reforms

There are five major benefits of the above proposals for reforming the state pension system and social security benefits:

1 By changing the relationship between means-tested benefit levels and compulsory pension provision, the proposals remove a disincentive to make pension provision.

2 The proposals halt and reverse the growth in the number of people affected by means testing, by removing the 'creep' of means-tested benefits up the income scale.

3 By combining the BSP and S2P, they considerably simplify the pensions system. A couple on low-to-medium incomes could reduce the number of different sources from which they receive income from six to one (ignoring council tax and housing benefit). The number of marginal tax and benefit withdrawal rates will be reduced and marginal tax and benefit withdrawal rates themselves will be reduced over a considerable portion of the income spectrum.

4 The proposals will considerably reduce the regulatory burden on pension schemes without making basic benefits less

secure. There will also be a commensurate decrease in the costs to the government of running the pensions system and regulating the contracting-out process.

5 There will be increased opportunities for private provision and simpler processes for contracting out of the state scheme.

14 CHANGES TO THE TAXATION OF PENSIONS

The taxation of pension funds

In Part 2 we pointed out that the tax system for pensions is economically incoherent and does not seem to achieve any clear objective. Two particular problems are the exemption of equity investments from the general rule that investment returns in a pension fund are tax free, and the tax-free lump sum which discourages annuity purchase and is, more generally, an anomaly.

In the past, exempt approved pension funds received a tax credit on dividends from UK companies, so equity investments were partly tax free. The July 1997 Budget, however, removed the dividend tax credit. This both discourages pension funds from investing in equities and encourages corporations to have more highly geared, debt-financed balance sheets. Neither of these results is likely to be economically beneficial, and the latter one, in particular, could be seriously harmful.

The calculations in Part 2 and Appendix B show that the tax-free lump sum reduces the cost of funding a given net pension by roughly the amount that the removal of the tax credit on dividends increases the cost of funding a given net pension. Removing the partially tax-free status of dividends in pension funds is estimated to have gained the Exchequer about £5 billion p.a. in revenue. The Inland Revenue could remove the two distortions of the tax-free lump sum and the over-taxation of equity investments and produce a more coherent system, with little net tax cost in present-value terms. Thus we propose that the tax-free lump sum should be abolished and the tax credit on dividends restored.[1]

There would be some practical problems with this reform. One could not expect the tax cost of restoring the tax credit on dividends to be coincident with the increased tax receipts from abolishing the tax-free lump sum, quite apart from having to manage the process of removing a benefit to which many people are attached.[2] Particular individuals close to retirement may also be adversely affected. We do not deny the public finance issues that such problems would raise. Even the full £5 billion cost of the tax credit, however, is only 0.5 per cent of GDP, and at least some, if not all, of this cost would be immediately balanced by introducing the taxation of the lump sum.[3]

If equity returns were to be *totally* tax free in pension funds, they would have to receive a tax credit for tax-free investors equal to the rate of corporation tax (30 per cent) paid on all profits earned by companies, not just on companies' distributions through dividends. Some form of imputation system would have to be used to ensure that non-taxpaying shareholders could reclaim such a credit. This might be expected to cost the Exchequer about £15 billion p.a. We would not regard this approach as practicable unless there was a complete reform of the corporation

---

1   This would not lead to equities being fully tax free (see Appendix B) but merely restore their pre-1997 position.

2   If people properly understood the regressive nature of the tax benefits associated with the lump sum, however, and the often poor value the lump sum offers when the pension has had to be commuted, it might lose some of its appeal.

3   People could still be permitted to take part of their pension fund as a lump sum, subject to tax and minimum annuitisation rules (see below).

tax system to move to a full imputation system – something that could be regarded as desirable but is well beyond the scope of this monograph.

We would therefore propose a phasing out of the tax-free lump sum and a restoration of the tax credit for pension fund equity investment. If this were done, one of the main ways in which pension saving can be abused for tax purposes would be removed. It would no longer be possible to manipulate pensions saving, particularly when close to retirement, in order to obtain tax relief on contributions and then a tax-free lump sum. The Inland Revenue could therefore become much more relaxed about particular abuses of the pensions system and this would enable them to abolish further regulations limiting pension provision. The restoration of the tax credit would also help restore the neutrality of the tax system with regard to different categories of investments.

Administrative reform: reducing the number of tax codes

The Inland Revenue's consultation documents (Inland Revenue, 2002, 2003) proposed a single tax code for all pension schemes, which we welcome. The framework for the new regime, which will come into force from 6 April 2006, has been set out in the Finance Act 2004. The Act removes some of the haphazard divisions between personal pensions, occupational defined contribution and occupational defined benefit schemes. Concurrent membership of these arrangements will be extended to everyone and the limits on contributions and benefits will affect only the few most well-off contributors. The basic principle of the government's proposals is that, during his or her lifetime, a prospective pensioner can make whatever arrangements in a 'registered pension scheme' are deemed suitable without limits, although contributions above an Annual Allowance (100 per cent of pay or £215,000 in 2006/7) will be taxed. At the time of retirement, the value of any registered pension in payment, or coming into payment, will be assessed. If the total is above a pre-set 'Lifetime Allowance', which will be £1.5 million in 2006/7, the individual will be taxed at 55 per cent on the excess.

These proposals do allow simplification but may still cause confusion at the limit, although this will be a problem only for the highly paid. A tax liability could arise, for example, if there were a sudden change in investment values close to retirement which took an individual's pension investments above the pre-set limit. There are special rules to establish equivalent values of defined benefits with defined contribution savings. Since the aim was 'simplicity', little distinction is made between different types of defined benefit scheme, which gives those whose employers are prepared to spend the money on them opportunities to play the system.

It is important that more people are not affected by the £1.5 million total pension benefit that can be received, as the administration of this limit will cause some complexity. We therefore propose that it is indexed in legislation to the increase in the retail price index each year plus 2 per cent, so that it falls only slowly, if at all, relative to average salaries.

The new rules also do nothing to reduce the reams of Department for Work and Pensions (DWP) legislation that distinguishes between personal pensions, occupational defined contribution and defined benefit provision, and places obstacles in the way of employers making appropriate and affordable provision for their employees. Such rules should be unnecessary, given our proposed changes to the state pensions system.

Overall, we believe that the Inland Revenue simplification is a major improvement, particularly the extension of concurrent membership to all employees. Further simplification and consequent reduction in government tinkering, however, would be possible if the tax-free lump sum were abolished. It is also worth noting that the authors have argued for an alternative form of simplification (discussed in Booth and Cooper, 2003) that involves allowing concurrent membership of different schemes with liberal benefit limits on any defined benefit provision and liberal contribution limits on defined contribution provision, together with an abolition of the tax-free lump sum. The limits on contributions would be effective in the year a contribution is made so there would be no need for a potentially bureaucratic and perhaps speculative comparison of defined benefit and defined contribution pensions at a future retirement date. If the proposal for up-rating the £1.5 million limit on total benefits were accepted, however, we would be equally happy with the Inland Revenue's changes, given that limits on tax-relieved pension provision will apply to very few people.

Annuitisation rules

Annuitisation rules are the rules that require individuals to take their pension benefits as annuities and restrict the particular form of the annuity that is taken. These are part of the regulatory system surrounding pensions because they are designed to prevent pension schemes, with their particular tax structure, being used for general savings. The current rules regarding the annuitisation of pension benefits militate against the achievement of legitimate economic objectives.

The two most obvious economic objectives of policy towards annuitisation should be:

1   to prevent moral hazard, by preventing individuals from taking their retirement savings as cash and then claiming means-tested social security benefits; and, once this has been achieved,
2   to allow maximum economic freedom for annuitants to arrange their pension income as best befits their own circumstances.

Thus the system should require some minimum annuitisation and then allow maximum freedom. Currently, it does the opposite, allowing freedom as to how the first 25 per cent of benefits is used and then prescribing how all the rest of the benefits should be used. The current system encourages taking benefits as cash when the individual may not have enough pension to be free of social security benefits and then prevents pensioners taking benefits as cash even where they have income well above the social security level. It should be noted that freedom to take benefits as cash, once some minimum annuitisation has taken place, would also allow individuals to purchase insurances (e.g. health or long-term care insurance) with part of their pension savings; it would also mean that an individual in poor health would not have to fully annuitise a pension fund.

Assuming the abolition of the tax-free lump sum, our framework for annuitisation rules would be very simple. Individuals would be required to use their tax-relieved pension savings to purchase insured, price-index-linked annuities (either joint or single life) such that their insured annuity income (including state pension, if any) would be 1.5 times the state's minimum social security benefit.

Non-annuitised parts of pension savings could be taken in cash at any time, subject to the rules of the schemes that individuals have joined, but income tax would be payable on any income withdrawn at any time and there would be a tax charge on any money left in the fund at death. Housing and council tax benefit (and pension credit above the guarantee credit level), if these benefits are to remain, would not be paid to an individual unless at least 90 per cent of the total pension pot had been annuitised at some time before such benefits were claimed. Investment returns would continue to be earned on the same tax basis as used for pension funds more generally on any capital not annuitised.

Equivalent rules would have to apply to defined benefit schemes. For example, individual members could be required to take all benefits as an annuity until the annuities totalled 1.5 times the guarantee credit (or minimum subsistence income support payment). If the member wished, the cash equivalent of any remaining benefits could be paid to a defined contribution pension provider and treated as though it had arisen as a defined contribution benefit. It is possible that trustees might not be prepared to accept the costs and risks of operating such a flexible system – but that would simply be a matter of the contractual arrangements between the member and the employer.

15 THE RETIREMENT AGE

Some economic considerations

Suppose there were no institutional or governmental influences on retirement decisions and individuals could accumulate their own savings for retirement in defined contribution pension schemes. Then, at any age, individuals could consider the amount in their retirement funds and the price of annuities and decide whether they wished to retire or to carry on saving. A number of factors would affect that decision: for example, the level of salaries; the rate of return on their funds if they continued to be invested; and levels of mortality, which would help determine annuity prices. If economic or demographic variables change, potential pensioners would be free to change their decisions, reacting to changes in relative prices such as wages and the return on capital. For example, if labour were in short supply and wages rose, retirement might be deferred. Similarly, if longevity continued to improve, annuity prices might rise and people could respond by working longer. If the opportunities were available, individuals might choose partial retirement, for example by taking part of the fund as an annuity and continuing in part-time employment. The market can adjust, at least in part, to ameliorate the impact of changing demographics on labour supply, asset prices, investment returns, and so on.

Removing perverse incentives

Governments put a number of institutional constraints in the way of such freedom and institutionalise particular retirement ages. Such constraints include:

- relatively rigid rules about the age from which the state pension can be drawn – these are being relaxed;
- tax rules that restrict the freedom of choice as to how an annuity is purchased with a pension fund;
- the provision of means-tested benefits, which reduce the incentive to work after a particular age, particularly since the system of benefits is different after state pension age is reached;
- rules applying to occupational schemes that make partial retirement difficult – these are also in the process of being relaxed;
- the system of incapacity benefit – although this is beyond the scope of this monograph.

It is possible that defined benefit schemes (both in the public and the private sectors) also restrict the choice of retirement age and have been used by employers to facilitate early retirement. While retirement age can be flexible in these schemes, partial retirement is more difficult than in defined contribution schemes (even if permitted by the Inland Revenue) and individuals do not have the freedom of decision that they have with defined contri- bution schemes (they have traded that freedom for increased security). We do not consider these issues further. Defined benefit schemes result from a free contractual arrangement between employer and employee, and such arrangements may be optimal *ex ante* for particular individuals and groups even if they lead to apparently undesirable consequences *ex post* in certain situations.

However, the state can enable greater flexibility. We have already proposed that the state pension age should be abolished and replaced by a 'reference age' at which a standard level of state retirement benefit could be calculated (we have suggested age 70, and the age could increase as longevity improves). Individuals could be allowed to draw state retirement pension from other ages with an actuarially adjusted pension being paid. It would be relatively straightforward to relax Inland Revenue and DWP rules to allow more freedom as to the form in which an income in retirement could be drawn, given the proposals that we have made regarding changes to annuitisation rules (see Chapter 14). Dealing with the systems of means-tested benefits may be more difficult politically. As life expectancy increases, however, it will be seen as increasingly anachronistic to treat individuals above the age of 65 as if they are incapable of working when means-tested benefit entitlements are determined.

Retirement at age 65 is encouraged because the high benefit withdrawal rates reduce incentives to work (see Part 1). High levels of post-retirement social security benefits encourage individuals to retire before 65 too. While an individual's state retirement pension must be taken at age 65 or later (for women as well as for men after 2020) some other pension benefits and all other personal savings can be drawn down earlier. If the pension benefits an individual expects at age 65 are projected to be less than the level of weekly income at which the Pension Credit plus other means-tested benefits stop, there is an incentive to ensure that other income and assets are minimised in the post-65 period. A rational individual could therefore retire early (the earliest age at which people can draw on their pension savings is 50[1]) and use up as much as possible of their non-pension and pension savings before age 65 to maximise their entitlement to means-tested benefits after age 65.

The purposes of social security payments and those of pensions systems have been confused in public policy. The main purpose of social security is to provide those without a basic income with the means to live at a given standard of living. It is not unreasonable that the level of basic income is determined through the democratic process: even many of the most liberal economic states have a guarantee of basic income provision. It does not seem sensible, however, to adjust that minimum standard of living, which the state ensures everybody has, sharply upwards at a particular age (65). Providing annuity income from a given age to provide for a comfortable old age is the purpose of pensions systems. Of course, individuals' needs do increase as they become older (for example, the very elderly often require personal or nursing care), but these increased needs are more sensibly met through the provision of needs-based benefits.[2] Removing the distinction between the levels of means-tested benefits before and after retirement would go some way towards removing the incentives to retire at earlier ages.

Deinstitutionalising retirement ages

Individuals can defer taking their state retirement pension: payment can be deferred until age 70 and the pension paid will be

1   The Finance Act 2004 increases this to 55 from 2010.
2   Individuals could be allowed to contract out of such needs-based state insurance schemes.

increased to compensate. In theory, there should be three aspects to such a late retirement augmentation:

1 the pension is being received later so it should be increased to reflect interest that could have been earned on the pension not paid;
2 there should be a mortality adjustment because a proportion of people who defer will die before the pension is received; and
3 there should be an age adjustment because it is expected that the pension will be received for a shorter time.

The 2004 Pensions Act will introduce late-retirement adjustment factors that are slightly better than actuarially neutral to deal with the above three issues (i.e. there is an incentive for late retirement).[3] The late retirement adjustment is not effectively publicised, however – although this may change with the new provisions.

It could be argued that the state pension scheme also reduces economic freedom by discouraging *earlier* retirement. We have therefore also proposed that all state pension benefits and benefits bought with rebates from contracting out of the state pension could be taken at any age after 60 with appropriate reductions in pension to reflect earlier retirement as long as insured annuities have been purchased at 1.5 times the level of means-tested benefits.

3 The Pensions Act also introduces a lump-sum alternative to the augmented state pension, but the lump sum compensates only for the first of the three items above, so in many cases will provide less good value (although different tax and means-testing requirements will apply to the lump sum and pension, making the comparison unnecessarily complicated).

This proposal, combined with the proposal to remove the distinction between the levels of means-tested benefits paid before and after age 65, should help 'deinstitutionalise' retirement ages. It would allow people more freedom as to when they retired and allow them to choose the optimal mix of work and leisure at all ages. The state pension age would simply become a 'reference age' for the calculation of a particular level of pension. These issues are not merely academic – a recent OECD report (OECD, 2004) pointed out the importance of simplification of pensions and social security if the UK were to remove the incentives to early retirement (both before and after the current state pension age) that currently exist. The OECD suggested that such moves were vital to ensure that the older working population was not discouraged from labour market participation.

16 SIMPLIFYING THE TAXATION OF PERSONAL INCOME IN RETIREMENT

There is currently clear discrimination in the tax system whereby individuals below state pension age are treated differently from those above it. The nature of the economic distortions caused by this differential treatment is unclear. At the very least, however, they create 'paperwork' costs and their removal would simplify the tax system. In addition, some of the special tax concessions are withdrawn at particular income levels, leading to marginal rates of tax that vary considerably with income and are sometimes very high at moderate incomes. All the special features in the tax system for those over age 65 lead to them paying less tax (or not more tax) than those under age 65 at any given income level.

The personal allowance is age related, so that those aged 65 or over start paying tax only when their income exceeds £6,830 (in 2004/5) compared with £4,745 at younger ages. The tax allowance is then further increased to £6,950 at age 75.

Married couples can also claim a married couples allowance if one of them was born before 1935. This increases if either one of the couple is 75 or over. While there is room for debate as to whether there should be a married couples allowance or transferable tax allowances for families in general, there is no justification for a variable married couples allowance for those over a certain age only. The married couples allowance is also withdrawn when

Figure 9   **Marginal tax rates**

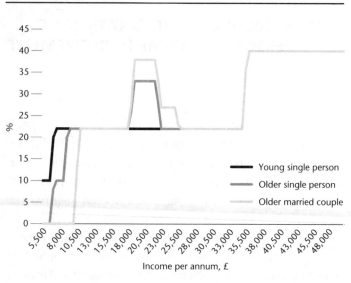

the couple's income exceeds £18,900 p.a. at the rate of 50 pence per pound of income until the withdrawal reaches £200, the value of the allowance, thus confusing the picture even further. This imposes a 33 per cent marginal tax rate on pensioners with incomes between £18,900 and £23,000. The marginal tax rates for pensioners are shown in Figure 9.

There is no economic justification for these special allowances and either they should be removed or tax allowances at younger ages should be increased.

The underlying question is: 'Why have a special tax system for the elderly?' The answer probably lies in public choice economics. A special tax system has been set up to benefit a particular group of people who, on average, have low incomes and who have a tendency to vote in general elections. The system also benefits pensioners on high incomes if they are able to structure their incomes in particular ways, but it does not help the non-aged poor.

A measure of the 'paperwork costs' imposed by these allowances is the page of the standard tax form and at least four and a half pages of the calculation guide (two and a half pages of which involve carrying out complex calculations) taken up by the age-related allowances. It should be noted that we have not superimposed the marginal tax rates on the marginal benefit withdrawal rates (see Figure 3) to show the complexity of the system in its totality. This complexity is almost impossible to illustrate pictorially!

We propose, quite simply, that there should be no special tax allowances for the elderly. The extent of any redistribution of income away from pensioners as a result of this policy will not be great – the cost of the tax allowances is about £1 billion, according to Curry and O'Connell (2003). The maximum possible benefit from this labyrinthine tax system to any particular pensioner is about £400.

17 CONCLUSION: THE POLITICAL ECONOMY OF AN END TO THE QUAGMIRE

In an age in which it is difficult to see the government not providing a basic subsistence income to the very poor, a minimum pension provision is proposed. This minimum provision is very limited in scope and very straightforward. There are alternative state and private mechanisms available so that nobody has to have any state pension provision if they do not wish to do so. There is significant scaling back of state means-tested and non-means-tested benefits proposed, with the removal of the discrimination between people of different ages. A coherent tax framework is proposed. Very few regulations are required because the system is designed to provide a framework for retirement provision and not dictate detailed outcomes. There are regulations proposed to ensure that defined benefit schemes are sufficiently solvent to meet minimum obligations and that they provide information to members about their level of solvency in respect of other benefits. There are also very limited regulations to prevent tax abuse.

Beyond this, the system would be free to evolve to meet the needs of prospective pensioners. It is impossible to predict the outcome of such a liberalised system. Formal pension provision might, in fact, fall. The abolition of the tax-free lump sum might encourage some people to use other forms of saving or pay down their mortgages or other debts, once the compulsory minimum pension provision had been made. Alternatively, the increased freedom that individuals have to use their pensions saving as they see fit may lead to the evolution of schemes with different forms of benefit attached or which combine various forms of insurance with pension provision. We would argue that the government should not worry about these kinds of issues as long as there are incentives – or, strictly speaking, no artificial disincentives – to individuals to pursue purposefully their own diverse objectives using the various savings, pensions and insurance vehicles that are available or become available in a liberalised market.

Our proposals create a straightforward pensions framework with a much-reduced and carefully defined role for the state. Even those who believe in significant government intervention in providing retirement income may well welcome the proposals because they are likely to enable the state to fulfil its more carefully defined role more effectively than it currently fulfils its complex and frequently contradictory roles. The framework would be robust in the face of changing economic conditions because it is built on enduring and simple principles. The framework is as impervious to rent-seeking by those looking to gain a higher income from the state or from professionals who are the beneficiaries of more complex regulation and social security systems as any framework that leaves a role for the state could be.

We finish by discussing whether our proposals take the UK pension system in a more market-oriented direction and whether they increase the efficacy of market provision.

Proposed changes to the taxation of pension funds (removing the tax-free lump sum and largely restoring the tax-free nature of equity returns) would unambiguously move the pensions tax system in a market-oriented direction. Significant tax distortions relating to corporate financing decisions and individuals' pension provision would be removed. It is difficult to see any welfare loss from implementing these proposals.

Simplified tax codes will remove significant amounts of regulation from individuals and pension schemes and allow greater freedom for individuals to decide the mix of market vehicles they use for pension provision (as acknowledged by the Inland Revenue, 2002, 2003). Furthermore, the proliferation of vehicles created simply to comply with different tax codes and the associated regulation could be reversed.

Proposals regarding annuitisation would increase freedom of choice as to how retirement funds were used, removing regulatory constraints on the development of market instruments for retirement provision. Again, significant deregulation would be possible.

The removal of a range of state benefits and the merging of two state pensions would not directly increase the role of the market in retirement decisions as such but would remove various aspects of micro-management of individuals' incomes which can impose costs (if only paperwork costs) on claimants and the government. Simplification of the tax system applying to pensioners would have the same effect and would make the tax system more neutral.

Proposals have also been made to reduce significantly the regulatory burden on occupational pension schemes. In particular, two specific economic functions of regulation have been identified (the problem of moral hazard in relation to those benefits that form part of the compulsory minimum provision and possible information asymmetries with regard to other benefits) and a light degree of regulation is proposed to address these problems.

Finally, we have made proposals that relate to the funded/ unfunded debate, a debate that we have, in other respects, circumnavigated. The opportunity exists for more private provision because of the merging of the two state pensions and by allowing individuals to contract out of the merged pension (rather than just one of the state pensions, as is the case at the moment). A wider range of individuals would also be allowed to contract out of the state scheme, and it should be possible to allow individuals to have any state accrual to date 'bought out' in exchange for a transfer value to a private sector scheme. It should be noted, however, that one of the authors would prefer to have more constraints on the form of private provision that could be purchased with any rebates from the state scheme, and the other author would be content with further state withdrawal from pension provision.

Greater use of contracting out and the formalisation of an accruals system for all state pension provision would bring another important change to the political economy of the state pension scheme, the long-term importance of which should not be underestimated both in terms of the promotion of the market economy and also in terms of better public policy development. The ability to contract out of a state benefit, even if alternative private provision has to be made, is the equivalent of moving from the state provision of a service to a voucher system (where the state decides how much is spent on a service but does not necessarily provide the service).

An 'accruals basis', which means that in each year a fixed amount of pension is accrued,[1] should erode public choice incentives for groups to campaign for income transfers facilitated through the pension system. The accruals system would reduce

1   Although the accrued pension can be linked to an index such as price or wage increases or an index in between price and wage increases, as we have proposed.

the risk of increases in pension being made for specific groups (for example, for the current retired population), because their pension would already be defined. If pensions were increased for future accrual, rebates would have to be increased too – as would NICs, from which the rebates are financed. The group campaigning for the increased pension accrual rate would have to pay the cost of that increased accrual. This public choice argument is one very important reason why a contributory state pension (with private alternatives allowed) is superior to a 'citizen's pension' (see also Chapter 1).

The costs of state pensions as a whole could also be made more transparent by publishing future state pension liabilities as part of government debt, by requiring future state pension liabilities to be 'funded' through the purchase of government debt instruments and/or by having a separate NIC that is dedicated to funding pension provision. Thus it would become clearer still to the generation that voted for increased future pensions that they would be paying for them, although the more people who are receiving contracted-out rebates, the greater is the explicit and immediate cost of increasing the rate of pension accrual. .

Of course, the authors are not so naive as to believe that there will not be political pressure for income transfers from one group to another through tax concessions, means-tested benefits or adjustments to the pension system. By putting the pension system on a long-term sustainable footing, however, simplifying its links with means-tested benefits and making the whole system more transparent, political and interest group pressures should be reduced. Indeed, all the proposals in this monograph involve the stripping out of special privileges given to particular groups through the pensions, tax and benefits system which have created a rent-seekers' paradise. It would seem that such rent-seeking is the cause of the quagmire and thus any meaningful long-term reforms of the pensions system must address that problem at its root.

APPENDIX A: ESTIMATE OF COST OF PROVIDING MINIMUM INCOME GUARANTEE AND BASIC STATE PENSION

The calculations were based on men retiring aged 65 at the start of 2003 and in 2050. The annuities are based on their single life only and make no allowance for survivor benefits.

The benefits valued were:

- The Minimum Income Guarantee (MIG), which was £98.15 per week and is assumed to increase in line with earnings.
- The full single person's Basic State Pension (BSP), which was £75.50 per week and assumed to increase in line with prices.
- At retirement in 2050 a State Second Pension (S2P) of £113 per week (in 2003 prices). This assumes S2P becomes flat rate from 2009/10 (the original intention was that it should become flat rate from 2006/7).

Assumptions

Mortality:
- For retirement in 2003, actuarial tables PMA92 (born 1935)
- For retirement in 2050, actuarial tables PMA92 (born 1985)

Interest rates:
- Discount rate 4.42 per cent net of expenses
- Inflation 2.37 per cent

- Real earnings growth 2 per cent

Retirement in 2003:
- The cost of purchasing an annuity equal to the MIG would be £97,000
- The cost of purchasing an annuity equal to the BSP would be £60,000

Retirement in 2050:
- The cost of purchasing an annuity equal to the MIG would be £282,000
- The cost of purchasing an annuity equal to the BSP would be £68,000
- The cost of purchasing an annuity equal to the assumed S2P would be £119,000

All figures in constant purchasing power terms.

APPENDIX B: **COST OF TAX REGIMES**

Practical problems of TTE and TEE regimes

There is, in fact, a serious practical difficulty in using any tax system for pensions saving which taxes earnings contributed to the scheme (TTE or TEE). Logically, any such system would involve defining a 'taxable benefit' for each employee, equal to the employer's contribution to the scheme on the employee's behalf. This would be virtually impossible to calculate as the nature of defined benefit schemes is such that it does not attribute employer contributions to individuals. Given this problem, we have had to make various 'working assumptions', as explained below, when making comparisons between the current tax system and TEE and calculating the costs of different tax systems. These assumptions give rise to reasonable results which are compatible with similar results calculated in the case of defined contribution schemes (where such problems do not arise) in Booth and Cooper (2002). In order to make the benefits comparable in the four different tax regimes in both the regime we describe as 'post-1997' and that which we describe as 'pre-1997', the tax-free lump sum was used to purchase a life annuity, with tax due only on the interest component. Annuitising all benefits enables consistent comparisons of benefits to be made.

Table 4 **Tax regimes**

Post-1997	E T$^+$ T^{partial}	**current regime**, dividend tax credits cannot be reclaimed.
Pre-1997	E T^{partial} T^{partial}	**pre-July 1997 budget regime**, same as the current regime but with tax credits available at a rate of 20% on dividends paid on UK equities.
Comprehensive income tax	TTE	**pure comprehensive income tax system**. No tax relief is given on contributions: contributions are adjusted so that net income remains the same. For simplicity we have assumed that 20% tax is levied on all investment returns except for UK equity returns and US equity returns, which are both assumed taxed at source at the corporation tax rate, with no further tax due.
Pure expenditure tax	EET (subject to caveat re US equities)	**pure expenditure tax regime** with the tax collected at the 'back end': full relief given on contributions; no tax paid on investment income. Dividends and UK equity returns arising from capital gains are both grossed up at the rate of corporation tax.[1] The lump sum is used to purchase a pension annuity, which is then taxed, rather than a life annuity taxed only on the interest component. This regime is EET except that withholding tax cannot (by virtue of the current UK/US double tax treaty) be reclaimed in respect of US equities.

---

1   Conceptually, this is a difficult issue. It is clear that dividends should be grossed up at the rate of corporation tax. Should capital gains be grossed up, however? The argument for grossing up capital gains is that one source of capital gains is the retention of profits that have been taxed at the corporation tax rate. Capital gains may, however, arise for other reasons as well. In theory, we should split capital gains into those arising as a result of profit retention and those arising as a result of changes in equity values for other reasons. This would not be practical, however, given publicly available data.

Description of tax regimes

The tax regimes used in our calculations are described in Table 4.

We assumed that the general income tax regime, in particular the tax rates and thresholds, was that in force for 2003/4. That regime includes the statutory provision that the main tax thresholds will be indexed annually in line with prices. While this statutory provision has on occasions been overridden in the Finance Act, price indexation is broadly what has happened for some years. The results are sensitive to this assumption, however.

Investment return and salary assumptions

In the model scheme used, members have a variety of salary patterns, with 42 per cent of the membership paying tax at the higher rate. The salary pattern is typical of an 'average' scheme although, of course, salary patterns in real-life schemes vary considerably depending on the nature of the industry and firm.

The asset allocation assumptions are shown in Table 5. Again, this is typical of the asset mix of defined benefit schemes.

Table 6 shows the investment-return figures that were used for all asset categories under the different tax regimes. The rationale for these figures is explained in detail in Booth and Cooper (2002). In summary, reasonable prospective estimates have been used, assuming inflation of 2.5 per cent p.a., for future nominal investment returns. The returns have then been adjusted to produce net returns on different tax bases. The results for the cost of providing pensions do, of course, vary, as investment return assumptions vary. The relative cost of funding pensions under different regimes, however, does not vary much if the gross investment return assumptions are changed.

Table 5 **Assumed asset mix of model scheme**

Investment category	Proportion of fund invested in category (%)
UK equities	55
US equities	15
Property	10
Index-linked bonds	6
Conventional bonds	10
Cash	4

Table 6 **Net investment returns under different tax regimes (per cent)**

Investment category	Post-1997	Pre-1997	Comprehensive income tax	Pure expenditure tax
UK equities	6.9	7.6	6.9	8.6
US equities	6.1	6.1	6.1	6.1
Conventional gilts	5.2	5.2	4.2	5.2
Index-linked gilts	5.0	5.0	4.0	5.0
Property	8.1	8.1	6.5	8.1
Cash	4.7	4.7	3.8	4.7

We have assumed only a small equity risk premium and have also assumed that *net* property returns will be higher than UK equity returns. This is because we have estimated future expected returns from current yield levels rather than used historical returns, and because the tax position of property investment is considerably more favourable than that for equity investment, particularly in the post-1997 regime.

Practical difficulties with the comprehensive income tax calculations

In order to make the comparisons of the standard contribution rates under the different tax regimes, we assumed that the pension scheme would be adjusted to provide an equivalent level of benefits under each tax regime. Hence we took the gross benefit under a pure expenditure tax (EET) regime accrued up to the date of exit, whether due to death, retirement or withdrawal, and applied the appropriate rate of tax in order to arrive at the value of the net EET benefit. This value was the benefit assumed to be funded under the comprehensive income tax (TTE) regime (and would then be received without further deduction of tax). In certain technical respects (discussed in Booth and Cooper, 2000) this is an oversimplification. The necessity of making this simplification, however, merely illustrates the impracticability of applying a TTE system to a defined benefit pension fund.

Detail of model scheme

In order to make the results of the calculations most widely applicable a 'typical' final salary pension scheme was used, with the benefits derived from those most frequently observed by the Government Actuary's Department's survey (GAD, 2003). The model scheme has the following characteristics.

We assume that choices between benefits, such as the lump sum at retirement, or the ability to take a transfer value on withdrawal, have no effect on the financing of the scheme. That is, we assume that choices given to members take place at prices that are actuarially neutral to the funding of the scheme.

Membership information was gathered from a variety of sources in order to construct a membership that could be deemed typical of an established occupational pension scheme (for example, GAD, 2003; NAPF, 2002). The weighted average age of the active members is 41, and the membership is split between active members, deferred pensioners and pensioners in approxi-

Table 7 **Pension scheme benefits**

Category	Benefit
Normal pension age	65
Accrual rate	One sixtieth of final salary p.a.
Pensionable salary	Basic salary
Death-after-retirement spouse's pension	50% pension
Early retirement	6% p.a. reduction in pension
Post-retirement pension increases	Inflation
Death-in-service lump sum	4 times salary
Death-in-service spouse's pension	50% accrued service
Withdrawal benefit	Statutory minimum

mately the proportions 38, 25 and 37 per cent respectively.

Members' salaries were increased in line with the national average salary increase assumption (see above), together with a promotional salary scale that was chosen to give a salary profile similar to that of the employed population as a whole. The consequence is that the salary profile of the active members is relatively steep at younger ages and flat towards retirement.

The valuation method and basis

The projected unit method was used to value the liabilities and to calculate the standard contribution rate of the pension scheme. This method implicitly assumes that the membership profile of the scheme is stable with respect to age, past service and salary distributions. The standard contribution rate is effectively calculated as the cost arising in the year following the valuation date, in respect of liabilities accrued due to service completed in that year, allowing for future salary growth.

The rate at which liabilities have been discounted has been derived from the weighted average return from the investment

Table 8 **Valuation interest rates**

Tax regime	Valuation rate of interest (%)
Post-1997	6.5
Pre-1997	6.9
Comprehensive income	6.2
Pure expenditure	8.0

Table 9 **Inflation and other financial assumptions (per cent)**

Inflation	2.1
Real salary growth	2.0
Increases to pension in payment	2.1

fund after tax. The rates are shown below for the various tax regimes considered. No allowance has been made for the risk to the employer of not following a matched investment policy, as we are not attempting to estimate a 'risk-free' cost and this would complicate the illustration.

Standard tables were used for mortality before and after retirement, and assumptions consistent with the derivation of the membership were made for the rates of withdrawal and early retirement.

Contribution rates under different tax regimes

The standard contribution rates[2] are given in Table 10. As has been noted, we have adjusted the accrual procedure so that all tax regimes give rise to the same net benefit in retirement to enable direct comparisons between contribution rates under different

---

2   The standard contribution rate is the cost of providing the future accruing benefits of the members of the scheme, calculated according to the valuation method and assumptions chosen, and expressed as a percentage of pensionable salary.

Table 10 **Standard contribution rates under different tax regimes**

Tax regime	Standard contribution rates (%)
Post-1997	13.9
Pre-1997	12.7
Pure expenditure	9.8
Comprehensive income tax	13.0 (15.8)

tax regimes. We have had to make further adjustments to the comprehensive income tax regime, however, as the members of the scheme would either have to pay tax on income used to finance contributions (if the contributions are employee contributions) or (if the contributions are made by the employer) would have to pay tax on an attributed benefit in kind.[3] The tax that would have to be paid on contributions amounts to 2.8 per cent of salary, making the total contribution rate for the TTE system 15.8 per cent of salary (shown in brackets in Table 10 above). It is this higher figure which is relevant in all comparisons.

In all cases the standard contribution rate can be applied to the total gross salary of the active membership to obtain the annual amount of the standard contribution required by the pension scheme. These contribution rates represent the cost, as a percentage of salary, of funding a given benefit under different tax regimes. The implications of these different costs are discussed in Chapter 10.

---

3   Alternatively, the sponsoring company would not be able to deduct contributions to the scheme from profits before corporation tax was levied.

REFERENCES

ABI (2003), *Stakeholder Pensions – Time for a Change?*, Association
of British Insurers

Boleat, M. (1998), *Insurability and Welfare Risks*, paper presented
at the IBC 'Insurance and Welfare State' conference

Booth, P. M. (1998), 'The transition from social insecurity',
Economic Affairs, 18(1): 2–12

Booth, P. M. (1999), 'The problems with PAYGO pensions',
Journal of Pensions Management, 4(3): 229–42

Booth, P. M. and D. R. Cooper (2000), *The Tax Treatment of
Pensions*, Actuarial Research Paper no. 122, London: City
University

Booth, P. M. and D. R. Cooper (2002), 'The tax treatment of UK
defined contribution pension schemes', *Fiscal Studies*, 23(1)

Booth, P. M. and D. R. Cooper (2003), 'Simplifying the taxation
of pensions', *Economic Affairs*, 23(3): 46–52

Booth, P. M., D. R. Cooper and G. Stein (2000), *The Impact of
Demographic Change*, London: Department of Trade and
Industry Foresight Panel

Booth, P. M. and G. Dickinson (1997), *The Insurance Solution*,
European Policy Forum

Brown, R. L. (1995), 'Paygo funding stability and
intergenerational equity', SCOR Notes, SCOR

Buchanan, J. M. (1978), *The Economics of Politics*, Readings 18, London: Institute of Economic Affairs

Chand, S. K. and A. Jaeger (1996), *Ageing Populations and Public Pension Schemes*, International Monetary Fund Occasional Paper no. 147, IMF

Clark, T. (2001), *Recent Pensions Policy and the Pensions Credit*, Briefing Note 17, Institute for Fiscal Studies

Cooper, D. R. (1997), 'Providing pensions for UK employees with varied working histories', *Journal of Actuarial Practice*, 5

Cooper, D. R. (2004), 'The pros and cons of contracting out of the State Second Pension', *Financial Adviser*, May

Cooper, D. R., D. Lewis and A. Smith (2003), *W(h)ither State Pension Age*, Staple Inn Actuarial Society

Curry, C. and A. O'Connell (2003), *The Pensions Landscape*, Pensions Policy Institute Reference Manual, Pensions Policy Institute

Daykin, C. D. (1998), 'Complementary pensions in the European Union', *Economic Affairs*, 18(1): 18–23

Daykin, C. D. (2002), *Pensions Systems: The EU and Accession Countries Lessons for the UK*, Politeia

De Ryck, K. (1996), *European Pension Funds: their impact on European capital markets and competitiveness*, European Federation for Retirement Provision

Deacon, A. (ed.) (2002), *Debating Pensions: Self-interest, citizenship and the common good*, Institute for the Study of Civil Society

DSS (Department of Social Security) (1998), *A New Contract for Welfare: Partnership in Pensions*, Cm. 4179, London: HMSO

DSS (Department of Social Security) (2000), *The Pension Credit: A consultation paper*, Cm. 4900, London: HMSO

DWP (Department for Work and Pensions) (2002), *Security, Simplicity and Choice: working and saving for retirement*, DWP Green Paper, Cm. 5677, London: HMSO

Emmerson, C. and S. Tanner (2000), 'A note on the tax treatment of private pensions and individual savings accounts', *Fiscal Studies*, 14(1): 42–56

Fabian Society (1990), *The Reform of Direct Taxation, Report of the Fabian Society Taxation Review Committee*, London: Fabian Society

Feldstein, M. (1987), 'Should social security be means tested?', *Journal of Political Economy*, 95(3): 468–84

Friedberg, L. (1999), *The Labor Supply Effects of the Social Security Earnings Test*, NBER Working Paper no. W7200

Friedman, M. and R. Friedman (1980), *Free to Choose*, London: Secker and Warburg

Friedman, M. and R. D. Friedman (1985), *The Tyranny of the Status Quo*, Harmondsworth: Pelican

GAD (2003), *Occupational Pension Schemes – 11th survey by the Government Actuary*, London: HMSO

Gruber, J. and D. A. Wise (eds) (1999), *Social Security and Retirement around the World*, National Bureau of Economic Research, Chicago, IL: University of Chicago Press

Hagemann, R. P. and G. Nicoletti (1989), *Population Ageing: Economic Effects and Some Policy Implications for Financing Public Pensions*, Economic Studies no. 12, OECD

Hannah, L. (1986), *Inventing Retirement: The Development of Occupational Pensions in Britain*, Cambridge: Cambridge University Press

House of Lords (2003), *Aspects of the Economics of an Ageing Population*, vol. ii, 'Evidence', Select Committee on Economic Affairs, London: HMSO

Inland Revenue (2002), *Simplifying the Taxation of Pensions: Increasing choice and flexibility for all*, London: HMSO

Inland Revenue (2003), *Simplifying the Taxation of Pensions: The government's proposals*, London: HMSO

Kay, J. A. and M. A. King (1990), *The British Tax System*, 5th edn, Oxford: Oxford University Press

Kenc, T. and W. Perraudin (1997), 'European pension systems: a simulation analysis', *Fiscal Studies*, 18(3): 249–77

Kessler, D. (1996), *Preventing Conflicts between the Generations*, 20th Annual Lecture of the Geneva Association

Knox, D. (1990), 'The taxation support of occupational pensions: a long-term view', *Fiscal Studies*, 11(4): 29–43

Knox, D. (1998), 'Australia's retirement income system', *Economic Affairs*, 18(1): 34–9

Kumar, A. and D. Ward (1999), *PENSIM: Developing Dynamic Simulation*, Government Economic Service Working Paper no. 136, London: DSS

Le Grand, J. and P. Agulnik (1998), 'Tax relief and partnership pensions', *Fiscal Studies*, 19(4)

Lunnon, M. (1996), *The Actuary*, London: Staple Inn Actuarial Society

Meade, J. E. (1978), *The Structure and Reform of Direct Taxation*, London: George Allen and Unwin

Miles, D. (1999), 'Modelling demographic change upon the economy', *Economic Journal*, 109(452): 1–36

Minford, P. (1998), 'The economic principles of pension provision', *Economic Affairs*, 18(1): 13–17

NAPF (2002), *Annual Survey*, London: National Association of Pensions Funds

Neumark, D. and E. Powers (1998), 'The effect of means tested income support for the elderly on pre retirement saving: evidence from the SSI program in the US', *Journal of Public Economics*, 68

Neumark, D. and E. Powers (1999), 'Means testing social security', in O. Mitchell, R. Myers and H. Young (eds), *Prospects for Social Security Reform*, Pension Research Council

O'Connell, A. (2003), *A Guide to State Pension Reform*, Pensions Policy Institute discussion paper

O'Connell, A. (2004), *Citizen's Pension: Lessons from New Zealand*, Pensions Policy Institute discussion paper

OECD (2004), *Ageing and Employment Policies: The United Kingdom*, Paris: Organisation for Economic Cooperation and Development

ONS (2004), *Living in Britain, Results from the 2002 General Household Survey*, London: HMSO

Paribas (1995), 'Economic brief', Paribas Capital Markets, 18 December

Parker, H. (ed.) (2002), *Modest but Adequate – a Reasonable Living Standard for Households Aged 65–74 Years*, Age Concern

Pickering, A. (2002), *A Simpler Way to Better Pensions*, independent report

Pinera, J. (1998), 'The Chilean model', *Economic Affairs*, 18(1): 24–33

President's Commission (2001), *Strengthening Social Security and Creating Personal Wealth for All Americans*, Report of the President's Commission to Strengthen Social Security, Washington, DC

Sefton, J., J. Dutta and M. Weale (1998), *Pension Finance in a Calibrated Model of a Saving and Income Distribution for the UK*, National Institute Economic Review no. 166

Seldon, A. (1960), *Pensions for Prosperity*, Hobart Paper 4, London: Institute of Economic Affairs

Simpson, D. (2003), 'How to clear up the pensions mess', *Economic Affairs*, 23(3): 11–15

Stein, G. (1997), *Mounting Debts: The Coming European Pension Crisis*, London: Politeia

Stroinski, K. (1998), 'Poland: the reform of the pensions system', *Economic Affairs*, 18(1): 29–33

SSSC (1999), *The Contributory Principle*, Report of the Social Security Select Committee, available from <www.parliament.uk/commons/selcom/socshome.htm>

Tullock, G., A. Seldon and G. L. Brady (2000), Government: Whose Obedient Servant? A primer in public choice, Readings 51, London: Institute of Economic Affairs

ABOUT THE IEA

The Institute is a research and educational charity (No. CC 235 351), limited by guarantee. Its mission is to improve understanding of the fundamental institutions of a free society with particular reference to the role of markets in solving economic and social problems.

The IEA achieves its mission by:

- a high-quality publishing programme
- conferences, seminars, lectures and other events
- outreach to school and college students
- brokering media introductions and appearances

The IEA, which was established in 1955 by the late Sir Antony Fisher, is an educational charity, not a political organisation. It is independent of any political party or group and does not carry on activities intended to affect support for any political party or candidate in any election or referendum, or at any other time. It is financed by sales of publications, conference fees and voluntary donations.

In addition to its main series of publications the IEA also publishes a quarterly journal, *Economic Affairs*, and has two specialist programmes – Environment and Technology, and Education.

The IEA is aided in its work by a distinguished international Academic Advisory Council and an eminent panel of Honorary Fellows. Together with other academics, they review prospective IEA publications, their comments being passed on anonymously to authors. All IEA papers are therefore subject to the same rigorous independent refereeing process as used by leading academic journals.

IEA publications enjoy widespread classroom use and course adoptions in schools and universities. They are also sold throughout the world and often translated/reprinted.

Since 1974 the IEA has helped to create a world-wide network of 100 similar institutions in over 70 countries. They are all independent but share the IEA's mission.

Views expressed in the IEA's publications are those of the authors, not those of the Institute (which has no corporate view), its Managing Trustees, Academic Advisory Council members or senior staff.

Members of the Institute's Academic Advisory Council, Honorary Fellows, Trustees and Staff are listed on the following page.

The Institute gratefully acknowledges financial support for its publications programme and other work from a generous benefaction by the late Alec and Beryl Warren.

Other papers recently published by the IEA include:

WHO, What and Why?
Transnational Government, Legitimacy and the World Health Organization
Roger Scruton
Occasional Paper 113; ISBN 0 255 36487 3
£8.00

The World Turned Rightside Up
A New Trading Agenda for the Age of Globalisation
John C. Hulsman
Occasional Paper 114; ISBN 0 255 36495 4
£8.00

The Representation of Business in English Literature
Introduced and edited by Arthur Pollard
Readings 53; ISBN 0 255 36491 1
£12.00

Anti-Liberalism 2000
The Rise of New Millennium Collectivism
David Henderson
Occasional Paper 115; ISBN 0 255 36497 0
£7.50

Capitalism, Morality and Markets

Brian Griffiths, Robert A. Sirico, Norman Barry & Frank Field

Readings 54; ISBN 0 255 36496 2

£7.50

A Conversation with Harris and Seldon

Ralph Harris & Arthur Seldon

Occasional Paper 116; ISBN 0 255 36498 9

£7.50

Malaria and the DDT Story

Richard Tren & Roger Bate

Occasional Paper 117; ISBN 0 255 36499 7

£10.00

A Plea to Economists Who Favour Liberty: Assist the Everyman

Daniel B. Klein

Occasional Paper 118; ISBN 0 255 36501 2

£10.00

The Changing Fortunes of Economic Liberalism

Yesterday, Today and Tomorrow

David Henderson

Occasional Paper 105 (new edition); ISBN 0 255 36520 9

£12.50

The Global Education Industry

Lessons from Private Education in Developing Countries
James Tooley
Hobart Paper 141 (new edition); ISBN 0 255 36503 9
£12.50

Saving Our Streams

The Role of the Anglers' Conservation Association in
Protecting English and Welsh Rivers
Roger Bate
Research Monograph 53; ISBN 0 255 36494 6
£10.00

Better Off Out?

The Benefits or Costs of EU Membership
Brian Hindley & Martin Howe
Occasional Paper 99 (new edition); ISBN 0 255 36502 0
£10.00

Buckingham at 25

Freeing the Universities from State Control
Edited by James Tooley
Readings 55; ISBN 0 255 36512 8
£15.00

Lectures on Regulatory and Competition Policy

Irwin M. Stelzer

Occasional Paper 120; ISBN 0 255 36511 X

£12.50

Misguided Virtue

False Notions of Corporate Social Responsibility

David Henderson

Hobart Paper 142; ISBN 0 255 36510 1

£12.50

HIV and Aids in Schools

The Political Economy of Pressure Groups and Miseducation

Barrie Craven, Pauline Dixon, Gordon Stewart & James Tooley

Occasional Paper 121; ISBN 0 255 36522 5

£10.00

The Road to Serfdom

The Reader's Digest *condensed version*

Friedrich A. Hayek

Occasional Paper 122; ISBN 0 255 36530 6

£7.50

Bastiat's *The Law*

Introduction by Norman Barry
Occasional Paper 123; ISBN 0 255 36509 8
£7.50

A Globalist Manifesto for Public Policy

Charles Calomiris
Occasional Paper 124; ISBN 0 255 36525 X
£7.50

Euthanasia for Death Duties

Putting Inheritance Tax Out of Its Misery
Barry Bracewell-Milnes
Research Monograph 54; ISBN 0 255 36513 6
£10.00

Liberating the Land

The Case for Private Land-use Planning
Mark Pennington
Hobart Paper 143; ISBN 0 255 36508 X
£10.00

IEA Yearbook of Government Performance 2002/2003
Edited by Peter Warburton
Yearbook 1; ISBN 0 255 36532 2
£15.00

Britain's Relative Economic Performance, 1870–1999
Nicholas Crafts
Research Monograph 55; ISBN 0 255 36524 1
£10.00

Should We Have Faith in Central Banks?
Otmar Issing
Occasional Paper 125; ISBN 0 255 36528 4
£7.50

The Dilemma of Democracy
Arthur Seldon
Hobart Paper 136 (reissue); ISBN 0 255 36536 5
£10.00

Capital Controls: a 'Cure' Worse Than the Problem?
Forrest Capie
Research Monograph 56; ISBN 0 255 36506 3
£10.00

The Poverty of 'Development Economics'

Deepak Lal

Hobart Paper 144 (reissue); ISBN 0 255 36519 5

£15.00

Should Britain Join the Euro?

The Chancellor's Five Tests Examined

Patrick Minford

Occasional Paper 126; ISBN 0 255 36527 6

£7.50

Post-Communist Transition: Some Lessons

Leszek Balcerowicz

Occasional Paper 127; ISBN 0 255 36533 0

£7.50

A Tribute to Peter Bauer

John Blundell et al.

Occasional Paper 128; ISBN 0 255 36531 4

£10.00

Employment Tribunals

Their Growth and the Case for Radical Reform

J. R. Shackleton

Hobart Paper 145; ISBN 0 255 36515 2

£10.00

Fifty Economic Fallacies Exposed
Geoffrey E. Wood
Occasional Paper 129; ISBN 0 255 36518 7
£12.50

A Market in Airport Slots
Keith Boyfield (editor), David Starkie, Tom Bass & Barry Humphreys
Readings 56; ISBN 0 255 36505 5
£10.00

Money, Inflation and the Constitutional Position of the Central Bank
Milton Friedman & Charles A. E. Goodhart
Readings 57; ISBN 0 255 36538 1
£10.00

railway.com
Parallels between the Early British Railways and the ICT Revolution
Robert C. B. Miller
Research Monograph 57; ISBN 0 255 36534 9
£12.50

The Regulation of Financial Markets
Edited by Philip Booth & David Currie
Readings 58; ISBN 0 255 36551 9
£12.50

Climate Alarmism Reconsidered

Robert L. Bradley Jr
Hobart Paper 146; ISBN 0 255 36541 1
£12.50

Government Failure: E. G. West on Education

Edited by James Tooley & James Stanfield
Occasional Paper 130; ISBN 0 255 36552 7
£12.50

Waging the War of Ideas

John Blundell
Second edition
Occasional Paper 131; ISBN 0 255 36547 0
£12.50

Corporate Governance: Accountability in the Marketplace

Elaine Sternberg
Second edition
Hobart Paper 147; ISBN 0 255 36542 X
£12.50

The Land Use Planning System

Evaluating Options for Reform

John Corkindale

Hobart Paper 148; ISBN 0 255 36550 0

£10.00

Economy and Virtue

Essays on the Theme of Markets and Morality

Edited by Dennis O'Keeffe

Readings 59; ISBN 0 255 36504 7

£12.50

Free Markets Under Siege

Cartels, Politics and Social Welfare

Richard A. Epstein

Occasional Paper 132; ISBN 0 255 36553 5

£10.00

Unshackling Accountants

D. R. Myddelton

Hobart Paper 149; ISBN 0 255 36559 4

£12.50

The Euro as Politics

Pedro Schwartz

Research Monograph 58; ISBN 0 255 36535 7

£12.50

Pricing Our Roads
Vision and Reality
Stephen Glaister & Daniel J. Graham
Research Monograph 59; ISBN 0 255 36562 4
£10.00

The Role of Business in the Modern World
Progress, Pressures, and Prospects for the Market Economy
David Henderson
Hobart Paper 150; ISBN 0 255 36548 9
£12.50

Public Service Broadcasting Without the BBC?
Alan Peacock
Occasional Paper 133; ISBN 0 255 36565 9
£10.00

The ECB and the Euro: the First Five Years
Otmar Issing
Occasional Paper 134; ISBN 0 255 36555 1
£10.00

Towards a Liberal Utopia?
Edited by Philip Booth
Hobart Paperback 32; ISBN 0 255 36563 2
£15.00

To order copies of currently available IEA papers, or to enquire about availability, please contact:

Lavis Marketing
IEA orders
FREEPOST LON21280
Oxford OX3 7BR

Tel: 01865 767575
Fax: 01865 750079
Email: orders@lavismarketing.co.uk

The IEA also offers a subscription service to its publications. For a single annual payment, currently £40.00 in the UK, you will receive every title the IEA publishes during the course of a year, invitations to events, and discounts on our extensive back catalogue. For more information, please contact:

Adam Myers
Subscriptions
The Institute of Economic Affairs
2 Lord North Street
London SW1P 3LB

Tel: 020 7799 8920
Fax: 020 7799 2137
Website: www.iea.org.uk